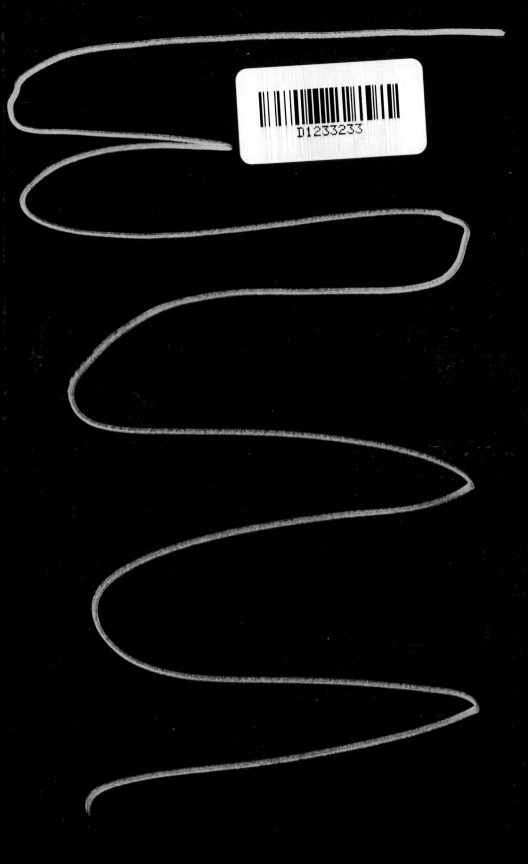
D1233233

THE GLOBAL FACE OF TERRORISM

BRENDAN JANUARY

TWENTY-FIRST CENTURY BOOKS / MINNEAPOLIS

Publisher's Note: To keep current on ISIS, follow reputable newspapers and other sources for breaking news and consult the Further Information section on pages 99–100 of this book for additional resources.

Text copyright © 2018 by Brendan January

All rights reserved. International copyright secured. No part of this book may be reproduced, stored in a retrieval system, or transmitted in any form or by any means—electronic, mechanical, photocopying, recording, or otherwise—without the prior written permission of Lerner Publishing Group, Inc., except for the inclusion of brief quotations in an acknowledged review.

Twenty-First Century Books
A division of Lerner Publishing Group, Inc.
241 First Avenue North
Minneapolis, MN 55401 USA

For reading levels and more information, look up this title at www.lernerbooks.com.

Main body text set in Adrianna Regular 11/15.
Typeface provided by Chank.

Library of Congress Cataloging-in-Publication Data

Names: January, Brendan, 1972– author.
Title: ISIS : the global face of terrorism / Brendan January.
Description: Minneapolis : Twenty-First Century Books, [2017] | Includes bibliographical references and index.
Identifiers: LCCN 2016036951 (print) | LCCN 2016050118 (ebook) | ISBN 9781512429985 (lb : alk. paper) | ISBN 9781512448658 (eb pdf)
Subjects: LCSH: IS (Organization)—Juvenile literature. | Terrorism—Religious aspects—Islam—Juvenile literature. | Terrorism—Middle East—History—Juvenile literature. | Islamic fundamentalism—Political aspects—Middle East—Juvenile literature. | Terrorism—Prevention—Juvenile literature.
Classification: LCC HV6433.I722 I85574 2017 (print) | LCC HV6433.I722 (ebook) | DDC 363.325—dc23

LC record available at https://lccn.loc.gov/2016036951

Manufactured in the United States of America
1-41598-23505-4/12/2017

WORTH PINKHAM
MEMORIAL LIBRARY
91 Warren Avenue
Ho-Ho-Kus NJ 07423

CONTENTS

1
Nightmare in Paris   4

2
Origins   16

3
From Insurgency to Caliphate   34

4
The Kingdom of God   52

5
Looking West   64

6
The Challenge of Our Times   78

Source Notes   90

Glossary   96

Selected Bibliography   98

Further Information   99

Index   101

1
NIGHTMARE
IN PARIS

inter was coming to the City of Light. It was
Friday night in Paris, in mid-November 2015.
Bars and restaurants were filled along the city's
elegant streets and boulevards. In the northern part of
the city, a raucous crowd packed the Stade de France
to watch the French national soccer team, dressed in
their royal blue jerseys, play a match against Germany.
France's president, François Hollande, was in the
stands.

At 9:20 p.m., a French midfielder skillfully used his
body to keep the ball from a German defender. Suddenly
a deep, muffled bang sounded from outside the stadium.
The crowd, thinking it a firework, broke into a ragged
cheer. The players didn't pause in their game.

French firefighters carry a wounded woman to safety outside the Bataclan nightclub in Paris, where ISIS jihadists killed eighty-nine concertgoers on November 13, 2015. In total, ISIS attacks in the city killed 129 and wounded more than 300 others that night.

A few minutes later, in the heart of the city, a black car pulled up outside a popular bar, Le Carillon. Bar patrons inside and at sidewalk tables were enjoying drinks and meals. The peaceful scene was shattered as two men emerged from the car, leveled Kalashnikov assault rifles, and began firing.

In a terrified scramble for cover, diners pressed against the sidewalk, dropped under tables, and hid behind chairs. Rounds of gunfire snapped loudly in the onslaught. The attackers moved from Le Carillon across the street to a Cambodian noodle shop, where they continued shooting. Fourteen victims died at both restaurants.

Back at the stadium, a French defender took a pass, and another explosion sounded. This one was louder, like a huge steel door swinging shut. The crowd cheered again. But a bodyguard soon leaned over Hollande's shoulder and whispered: *The country is under attack.*

The explosions had come from suicide bombers. They had planned to detonate their explosive vests inside the stadium amid thousands of fans. Instead, one man detonated his bomb at the stadium gate after a security guard prevented him from entering without a ticket. The explosion killed the bomber and a passerby. An accomplice, also unable to enter the stadium, detonated his vest outside a nearby McDonald's restaurant, killing only himself. Inside the stadium, security guards surrounded Hollande and rushed him to a motorcade. Sirens flashing, the motorcade sped off to a secure, undisclosed location.

Back at Le Carillon, bodies were sprawled on the sidewalk and in the street, cut down as they tried to flee. Gunfire sounded just a few blocks south, where the team of gunmen struck another café and then a restaurant. The restaurant's outdoor terrace became a killing field. In another part of the city, gunmen attacked an eatery called La Belle Équipe, killing nineteen.

At another restaurant, Comptoir Voltaire, a man nervously threaded his way among the closely spaced tables. He covered his face with his left hand and detonated a bomb strapped around his waist.

"VERY CALM, VERY DETERMINED"

At the city's Bataclan concert hall, an American heavy metal band, Eagles of Death Metal, was performing to a packed audience of fifteen hundred. Three men carrying assault rifles forced their way into the building. Crying "Allahu akbar" ("God is greater" in Arabic), they started shooting.

The music halted, and panicked concertgoers fled to upper boxes and crawled through windows. Michael O'Connor of Great Britain pulled his girlfriend toward an exit to the right of the stage. A crowd jammed the doorway. Behind the couple, the gunmen moved closer.

"People [were] falling all over the place, people screaming and just clawing and running and pushing to get away," O'Connor said. When the gunmen paused to reload their rifles, concertgoers dashed to the exits. But the gunmen were efficient. "When he started to shoot again, we just hit the floor. . . . I pulled my girlfriend underneath me and I lay on top of her. I thought I was going to die," said O'Connor.

Outside the hall, the staccato of automatic rifle fire drifted across the cityscape, joined by the scream of ambulances and emergency vehicles. Crumpled forms were scattered outside restaurants in ghastly positions amid overturned tables and glass windows chipped with bullet holes. Survivors, their faces etched with panic, horror, and shock, stumbled to safety. Near Le Carillon, residents threw down sheets to cover bloodied bodies in the street. Knots of police officers confronted crime scenes of unprecedented violence and savagery in a city that normally embodies elegance, beauty, and life.

Residents threw down sheets to cover bloodied bodies in the street. Knots of police officers confronted crime scenes of unprecedented violence and savagery.

Back in the Bataclan, the terrorists "were very calm, very determined," recalled one concertgoer. "They reloaded three or four times their weapons. . . . They were unmasked and wearing black clothes and they were shooting at people on the floor, executing them."

David Fritz-Goeppinger, a twenty-three-year-old Chilean-French photographer, watched one of the gunmen. "He had a gun in his hands. He fired, and he fired. And he laughed. There was a sort of triumph in death."

Desperate to escape, Fritz-Goeppinger climbed out a window and hung by his arms, high above the street. A terrorist spotted him and told him to come back in.

"He had a gun in his hands. He fired, and he fired. And he laughed. There was a sort of triumph in death."

—concertgoer at Paris's Bataclan nightclub

The gunman told Fritz-Goeppinger that "he had just killed 100 people and one more would not make any difference."

Fritz-Goeppinger climbed through the window and into the building. The terrorist looked over him. "I remember looking into his eyes, and he had beautiful blue eyes, blue like the sky, there was something magnificent about his eyes. The Kalashnikov was big. He said, 'Do you believe in God? Where is your God now?'"

The terrorist asked Fritz-Goeppinger his nationality. When he answered that he was Chilean, "there was something that was extinguished in their look, because I was a foreigner. He said, 'But you have an opinion about French politics?' And I said, 'No, no, no.'" Fritz-Goeppinger's frantic denial saved his life. He was astounded that a terrorist could kill people one moment and debate politics the next.

As police surrounded and entered the hall, the gunmen rounded up hostages, took them into a corridor, and placed them at doors and windows. The hostages became human shields. The police couldn't shoot into the corridor without killing them. After two hours, the police finally stormed the hallway. In an explosion of gunfire and stun grenades, the three terrorists were killed, but the hostages escaped injury.

Afterward, Paris reeled in shocked silence and horror. Nine terrorists had struck in a well-planned and coordinated attack, killing 129 people and wounding 352. "[The city] looked like a battlefield," said one survivor. "There was blood everywhere, there were bodies everywhere."

SYRIA, IRAQ, and SURROUNDING NATIONS, 2017

TURKEY

Dabiq

Aleppo

Raqqa

Mount Sinjar

Mosul

IRAN

SYRIA

Hawija

Tikrit

Palmyra

LEBANON

Euphrates River

N

Damascus

Mediterranean Sea

Ramadi

Baghdad

Daraa

ANBAR PROVINCE

IRAQ

Tigris River

JORDAN

Najaf

Miles
0   40   80
0 40 80 120
Kilometers

ISRAEL

SAUDI ARABIA

Persian Gulf

Based in Iraq and Syria, ISIS hopes to spread its extremist variation of Islam throughout the Middle East and beyond.

TRUE BELIEVERS

No one doubted who had carried out the attacks: the terrorist group ISIS, or the Islamic State in Iraq and Syria. Members of ISIS practice an extreme interpretation of Islam, a religion founded by the prophet Muhammad in the seventh century CE on the Arabian Peninsula. ISIS vows to wage jihad, or religious war, on anyone—Islamic or otherwise—who breaks what it believes to be the laws of God.

THE MANY NAMES OF ISIS

ISIS has many names. Originally it was called al-Qaeda in Iraq. It was the Iraqi branch of the al-Qaeda terrorist organization, founded in 1988 by Saudi Arabian jihadist Osama bin Laden. The group changed its name to the Islamic State in Iraq (ISI) in 2006. When ISI later spread into Syria, it added an *S* to its initials to become ISIS.

The US government calls the group ISIL, which stands for the Islamic State of Iraq and the Levant (the countries bordering the eastern Mediterranean Sea). The group refers to itself as the Islamic State (IS).

ISIS's Arabic-speaking enemies belittle the group by calling it Daesh (pronounced "dash"), an acronym for Arabic words that mean Islamic State in Iraq and Syria. The name is insulting because it sounds like the Arabic word for "stomp" or "scrub." In this book, to avoid confusion, we refer to the group as ISIS.

Many Muslims (practitioners of Islam) adhere to sharia law. This is Islamic law as written in the Quran, the Muslim holy book, and in the hadith, a collection of writings about the words and deeds of Muhammed. ISIS takes sharia law to the extreme. It believes in meticulously following the examples of Muhammad and his early followers in business, warfare, and family life. Under this radical interpretation of Islam, Muslims are obligated to destroy infidels, or nonbelievers. They are entitled to enslave the women and children of their enemies and to tax non-Muslims living under their rule. Following laws written in the seventh century, ISIS rejects much of the modern world. It particularly loathes the United States and western Europe, with their liberal attitudes about sex, drinking, gay rights, and women's equality.

ISIS punishes wrongdoers and enemies using techniques common in the seventh century: beheading, stoning, and crucifixion. ISIS believes that a caliphate—a territory ruled by a successor to Muhammad, according to sharia law—is the only valid form of government. It rejects democracy, political parties, political borders, and all non-Muslim governments.

Despite its extremist vision, ISIS has attracted followers from around the globe. It offers housing, health care, and other social services to the men and women who join its ranks, along with a sense of community and purpose. Many recruits, from the Middle East and elsewhere, see ISIS as a haven from unemployment, poverty, ethnic and religious persecution, and governmental corruption. Once they join, male recruits train as jihadists. They strike out at the group's enemies using terrorist tactics—bombings and shootings of civilian targets—as well as more traditional types of warfare.

Despite its extremist vision, ISIS has attracted followers from around the globe. It offers housing, health care, and other social services to the men and women who join its ranks, along with a sense of community and purpose.

THE FACE OF TERRORISM

ISIS emerged from the wreckage of the Iraq War (waged in Iraq by the United States and its allies between 2003 and 2011) and from a civil war in Syria that began in 2011. In its

To spread terror, ISIS frequently films executions and distributes the footage online. This image from an ISIS video released in August 2014 shows US journalist James Foley right before his beheading. The masked executioner, who had grown up in London, spoke on the video in English. The press nicknamed him Jihadi John.

brutal fight to create a caliphate, ISIS has conquered large areas of Iraq and Syria.

To fund its terrorist activities, ISIS has amassed a war chest in the hundreds of millions of dollars. The group resorts to many tactics. It confiscates money and goods from citizens in captured territories. Its fighters often take hostages, charging ransoms for their safe return. It executes the hostages if their families or governments don't pay up. ISIS captures valuable Middle Eastern oil wells and refineries, selling the oil on the international black market, an illegal network of buyers and sellers. It steals valuable and treasured antiquities (relics from ancient times), also selling them on the black market. In 2014, the peak year of its moneymaking activities, ISIS generated $1 million to $3 million a day.

ISIS has skillfully used modern technology, including social media and online video, to spread its message.

A CHILLING VIDEO

Two months after the Paris attacks, ISIS released a triumphant video. Filmed in high definition and slickly produced, it shows images of the aftermath of the attacks culled from US and European news organizations. It also features interviews with some of the terrorists, filmed before they traveled to Paris. On camera, dressed in camouflage battle gear, the men proudly read statements about their mission. Some of the men then execute kneeling prisoners—by gunshot or by a knife across the throat. One young man holds up a fist covered in fresh blood and grips a severed head. The rest of the dead body lies behind him. "Soon in [the] Champs-Elysées," he leers, referring to more murders to come on the grand and historic Parisian avenue. The video soundtrack then erupts with thunder and chanting.

"What are you doing?" another terrorist on the video asks of French Muslims. "We are out here killing the infidels. You're sitting there with your arms crossed. Take anything, take a rock, take your car, take a gun, take a knife and go kill the infidel in your street.... Kill them [infidels] wherever you find them."

After the attacks in Paris, French president François Hollande addressed citizens of his nation and others around the globe. He declared that "jihadism . . . threatens the whole world."

It puts out high-definition, well-produced videos with a rich mixture of content including fiery explosions and close-up interviews. Much of its propaganda features graphic images of extraordinary brutality, including massacres of prisoners, captives burned to death, and suicide bombings at religious buildings.

Since its founding in 2006, ISIS has supported, inspired, and carried out acts of terrorism around the globe. By early 2016, it had killed more than 1,200 people outside Iraq and Syria, in nations as far away as Australia, Denmark, the United States, and Bangladesh. Within Iraq and Syria, the death toll is much higher. In early 2016, the United Nations, an international peacekeeping and humanitarian organization, estimated that ISIS had killed more than 18,800 Iraqi and Syrian civilians in just two years. These victims were mostly Muslims.

The relentless campaign of violence and terror has forced the world to ask, what is ISIS? Where did it come from? Who joins and supports it? What do its members want? And how can ISIS be stopped? After the attacks in Paris, Hollande summed up the perils: "These assassins don't represent any civilization," he said. "We are in a war against terrorism, jihadism, which threatens the whole world."

2
ORIGINS

n early April 2003, columns of US tanks and armored
vehicles filled the highways leading to Baghdad, the
capital of Iraq. Smashed trucks and cars burned along
the roadside. Broken bodies lay scattered amid the
debris. Columns of smoke smudged the sky. The US
forces converged in the center of the city. Then US
troops pulled down a towering statue of Iraq's ruthless
leader, the dictator Saddam Hussein, as jubilant
Iraqis cheered.

This was the launch of the Iraq War, though its
origins can be traced to about a year and a half earlier.
On September 11, 2001 (9/11), nineteen members of the
Islamist terrorist group al-Qaeda—fifteen from Saudi
Arabia, two from the United Arab Emirates, and one
each from Egypt and Lebanon—had hijacked four US
passenger planes. The hijackers had steered two planes

A statue of Iraqi dictator Saddam Hussein stands behind a US Marine in the center of Baghdad. Soon after US troops entered the city, they attached ropes to the statue and used military vehicles to pull it down.

into the twin World Trade Center towers in New York City and one into the Pentagon, the US military headquarters outside Washington, DC. On the fourth plane, passengers fought the hijackers, who crashed the plane into a field in Pennsylvania. The highest death toll was in New York City, where the twin towers burned fiercely and collapsed in a thundering explosion of steel, glass, and concrete. By the end of the day, almost three thousand people were dead.

In the wake of the attacks, Americans were bewildered, terrified, and furious. No Iraqis had been involved in the 9/11 attacks. Nonetheless, US president George W. Bush argued that Iraq was a direct threat to the United States. With little evidence to support his claims, he charged that Iraq was building biological, chemical, and nuclear weapons that might be used in further terrorist attacks on US targets. He called for a US invasion of Iraq to remove Saddam Hussein from power and to set up a democratic government there. Many US citizens and global politicians backed Bush, while many others did not. Despite heated American and worldwide opposition, the US Congress authorized the invasion of Iraq in October 2002. The war began in March 2003. In April the US military seized Baghdad.

A few weeks later, Bush gave a speech on a US aircraft carrier off the coast of Southern California. He stood in front of a huge banner that read Mission Accomplished. As far as the Bush administration was concerned, the bulk of the fighting in Iraq was over and Saddam Hussein had been toppled. The United States had occupied the nation, with plans to set up a new government there. After decades of dictatorship, Iraqi citizens would vote for their own leaders in elections. At the White House, staffers discussed how long it would take for Iraq to become self-governing. Six months? A year? Most believed that US troops could come home soon.

Meanwhile, in Iraq, the US occupation wasn't going as well as planned. After Saddam Hussein's fall, Baghdad descended into looting, chaos, and lawlessness. The victorious Americans chose to disband the Iraqi army, worried that many Saddam Hussein loyalists were remaining among its ranks. While that was true, dismissing the army didn't make them less of a threat. Instead, even more Iraqi soldiers—trained in warfare and without pay or jobs—became eager recruits for a growing insurgency, a rebellion against the occupying US forces.

In the following months, insurgents attacked US troops with roadside bombs and sniper fire. They unleashed a string of devastating bombings against civilian targets. Truck bombs obliterated the Jordanian embassy and UN buildings in Baghdad, killing the UN's highest-ranking officer.

US Intelligence—military agents tasked with gathering information about the insurgents—searched to find out who had ordered the bombings. Among many clues, they discovered that the truck bombs had been built with similar munitions and wiring. Agents intercepted the same brief cell phone message—"Allah [God] was merciful today"—after each of the attacks. The clues led to a Jordanian terrorist nicknamed He Who Weeps a Lot because he shed tears when he read the Quran. His real name was Abu Musab al-Zarqawi.

US troops, Iraqi police, and Iraqi civilians stand near a destroyed car and burning debris in the aftermath of a truck bomb attack on the Jordanian embassy in Iraq in August 2003. By bombing the embassy, insurgents sent a message to other Middle Eastern nations that it wasn't safe to cooperate with the United States in creating a new government in Iraq.

"HERE WAS A REAL LEADER"

Al-Zarqawi, born in 1966, grew up in Jordan. As a youth, he was notorious for brawling, drinking, and petty crime. A short man, he had the tight, muscle-bound build of a natural fighter. He readily resorted to fists to get his way. His dark eyes and scowl radiated intensity.

His mother, worried about her son's behavior, steered him toward religion by taking him to the local mosque, or Islamic house of worship. To everyone's surprise, al-Zarqawi became a passionate convert. He attended daily prayers and joined a conversation group every week to discuss the Quran.

LINES IN THE SAND

Based in what became Turkey, the Muslim-led Ottoman Empire emerged in about 1300 and lasted until 1922. It was one of the most powerful empires in the world in the sixteenth and seventeenth centuries, when it controlled territory across the Middle East, North Africa, and parts of southeastern Europe. The empire had a robust economy, acclaimed universities, and strong artistic traditions.

The empire declined in the following centuries. During World War I (1914–1918), the Ottoman Empire linked itself with Germany and Austria-Hungary in an alliance called the Central powers. After the Central powers lost the war, victorious European nations carved the Middle East into separate territories and took control of them. The Europeans governed these lands with little consideration for the traditions, rights, interests, and political realities of the peoples who had lived there for centuries.

Later in the twentieth century, the Middle Eastern territories won their independence and became self-governing nations. But in many cases, European powers continued to exert great political and economic control over their governments. In the twenty-first century, ISIS is determined to unite the entire Middle East (and other parts of the world) under one caliphate, with no national borders. The caliphate would destroy what many historians have called the "lines in the sand" established by Europe in the Middle East after World War I.

In 1989 al-Zarqawi joined the jihad in the Muslim country of Afghanistan. Afghani jihadists (also called mujahideen) were fighting troops from the Soviet Union (a former nation of fifteen republics based in Russia from 1922 to 1991). The Soviets had invaded Afghanistan in 1979 to support that nation's pro-Soviet, Communist government. The mujahideen wanted to establish a government in Afghanistan based on

EUROPE, NORTH AFRICA, and the MIDDLE EAST, 2017

Since World War I, foreign powers, including the United States, the former Soviet Union (based in Russia), and many European nations, have exerted great political and economic control over the Middle East. In various wars and rebellions, Middle Easterners have fought to free themselves of this control.

Islamic teachings. (In the mid-1990s, a conservative Islamic group called the Taliban gained control of Afghanistan.)

After four years, al-Zarqawi returned to Jordan a committed jihadist. His life in Afghanistan had involved hardship, war, and camaraderie with other jihadists, all devoted to creating an orderly, Islamic-based society. In Jordan al-Zarqawi was dismayed by city streets full of liquor stores, pornography vendors, and women in revealing clothing—all of them in violation of strict Islamic teachings. al-Zarqawi believed that too many Muslims were ignoring sharia law.

Everything in Jordan excited his disgust. He scolded his mother and sister for not wearing the traditional burka, a hooded garment that many Muslim women wear to cover the body from head to toe. He yelled at his brothers for allowing their families to watch Western-style television shows—sitcoms and dramas similar to those shown in Europe and the United States.

Al-Zarqawi was not alone in his misery. Other Jordanians who had fought in Afghanistan felt a similar alienation and anger. They gathered, talked, brooded, and plotted against those they perceived to be the enemies of Islam. The Jordanian intelligence service was tracking many of them. Along with several colleagues, al-Zarqawi was arrested in 1994. He was convicted of possession of illegal weapons and sentenced to fifteen years in prison. In cramped jail cells, he bonded with a tight-knit group of other Islamist extremists.

Their leader was Abu Muhammad al-Maqdisi, a quiet man who spent his days reading the Quran and writing essays. Despite al-Maqdisi's demeanor, his essays were fierce. He went further than other Islamic scholars on a number of subjects. For example, he argued that Muslims had an obligation—even a duty—to kill their own leaders if they were "godless," or didn't rule their nations according to the most rigid interpretation of the Quran.

Al-Maqdisi argued that Muslims were obligated to defend themselves and to strike back against the "near enemy"—the corrupt Muslim leaders ruling many Middle Eastern countries at the time. He also argued that Muslims should strike out against the "far enemy." That meant the United States and European nations, which supported many corrupt Muslim-led governments in the Middle East.

If al-Maqdisi was the brain of the prison leadership, al-Zarqawi was the muscle. He enforced an unforgiving code of

This undated photo shows Abu Musab al-Zarqawi, who in the late 1980s and early 1990s took part in a jihad in Afghanistan. During the Iraq War, al-Zarqawi led the insurgency against Iraq's new US-backed government.

Islamic law on himself and the other Islamist inmates. While the prison allowed inmates to watch television, al-Zarqawi draped the screen with black cloth so that inmates would not see any un-Islamic images, such as a woman's uncovered body. Al-Zarqawi seldom smiled and never made small talk. He spent hours memorizing passages from the Quran. He demanded absolute obedience from his men, and he would physically punish anyone who stepped out of line. To maintain his physique, he piled stones into buckets for weight lifting.

To his mother and sister, al-Zarqawi expressed a softer side in a string of notes of love and affection, decorated with drawings of flowers. He would spend days before their visits cleaning and tidying his prison cell. He also became a frantic caretaker whenever any of his men were sick, watching over them and nagging the prison doctor about their care.

In March 1999, al-Zarqawi still had ten years left in his prison sentence when the king of Jordan died. As is customary in Jordan, the new king released a number of prisoners in a gesture of goodwill and mercy. Al-Zarqawi was among them. He spent his first night of freedom in his hometown with his mother. By five thirty the next morning, however, he was back at the prison to speak to his comrades still behind bars. He wanted to bolster their morale and make sure they did not feel he had abandoned them. "Here was a real leader," the prison doctor recalled. "I knew at that moment that I would be hearing about him. The man was going to end up either famous or dead."

Al-Zarqawi soon left Jordan and eventually made his way back to Afghanistan, where he met one of the top aides to Osama bin Laden, the leader of al-Qaeda. Bin Laden had formally declared war on the United States in 1996, decrying the presence of US forces in Saudi Arabia—the land where the prophet Muhammad had founded Islam. Bin Laden had also masterminded a series of attacks on US targets, including the 1998 bombings of the US embassies in Kenya and Tanzania, which had killed more than two hundred people. Expelled from his native Saudi Arabia for crimes against the government—and wanted by the United States for his terrorist attacks in Africa—bin Laden had taken refuge in Afghanistan. By then the Taliban ruled most of that nation. Bin Laden was welcome there.

With the support of the Taliban and money from al-Qaeda, al-Zarqawi established a training camp in eastern Afghanistan in 2000. Within eighteen months, he had attracted nearly fifty people to the camp. They included former jihadist contacts, fighters, and prison companions. He oversaw all activities at the camp—from prayer to training in the use of firearms.

After the September 11 attacks, the United States and its allies attacked al-Qaeda strongholds in Afghanistan, scattering al-Qaeda and Taliban fighters. Seriously wounded in a US bombing attack, al-Zarqawi fled Afghanistan for northeastern Iraq. There he was able to rally his tiny band. As he healed, he conceived a new hatred for the country that had almost killed him. When rumors spread of an impending US invasion of Iraq, al-Zarqawi felt a new certainty. "Iraq," he said, "will be the forthcoming battle against the Americans."

A WAR OF ALL AGAINST ALL

With the US invasion of Iraq, the "far enemy" had arrived. Al-Zarqawi was determined to ensure an American failure there through a long and bloody resistance. He pledged allegiance to al-Qaeda and became the leader of al-Qaeda in Iraq (AQI). He took his tactics from a document called *The Management of Savagery* by Abu Bakr Naji, the pen name of a suspected al-Qaeda strategist. The text instructed jihadists to use "a quantity of explosives that not only destroys the building [but] makes the earth completely swallow it up. By doing so, the amount of the enemy's fear is multiplied and good

> **"We must adopt a ruthless policy in which hostages are brutally and graphically murdered unless our demands are met."**
>
> —Abu Bakr Naji, *The Management of Savagery*

media goals are achieved." Naji also wrote, "We must adopt a ruthless policy in which hostages are brutally and graphically murdered unless our demands are met."

Al-Zarqawi was cunning as well as ruthless. By destroying the Jordanian embassy, he prevented Jordan—a stable Arab nation that might have given support, advice, and legitimacy to the US occupation—from establishing a presence in the new Iraq. After the bombing, other pro-US Arab nations also stayed away. And because of the attack on the United Nations, international agencies and humanitarian organizations did too.

It soon became clear that the US architects of the war in Iraq had acted rashly in their decision to occupy Iraq. Americans had little understanding of the many different groups that lived there, each with competing histories, loyalties, and interests. Iraq was less a nation of unified citizens than a collection of independent tribes. Most Iraqis are Muslims, but they belong to one of two different sects, or groups—the Shiites and the Sunnis. The split between Shiites and Sunnis occurred long ago, shortly after the prophet Muhammad died in the seventh century. With his death, his followers disagreed over who would lead the growing Muslim faith. The majority of Muslims (who became the Sunnis) united behind one caliph, while a smaller group (who became Shiites) backed another leader. In the twenty-first century, the Sunnis still make up a majority (about 90 percent) of the world's 1.5 billion Muslims.

In Iraq, by contrast, Sunnis are a minority of the country's population, but they had controlled the government and the army under Saddam Hussein, who was a Sunni. When US and allied forces overthrew Saddam Hussein, the Shiites—supported by neighboring Iran (a Shiite-majority nation)—moved quickly to assert leadership. US policymakers optimistically urged the new Shiite leaders to share power with the Sunnis and build a fair, secular (nonreligious) government that represented all Iraqis.

APOSTASY

Al-Zarqawi, a Sunni, had no intention of allowing that to happen. He planned to break Iraqi's secular society and institute his strict version of Islamic law in Iraq. In one of his most controversial acts, in 2005 al-Zarqawi defied Abu Muhammad al-Maqdisi over the question of apostasy—or deviation from Islamic teaching. For al-Maqdisi, apostates were only those who committed serious religious crimes, such as denying the perfection of the Quran. But al-Zarqawi's definition was much wider. In his eyes, anyone who dressed like a Westerner, endorsed or voted for a Western-backed government, or sold or consumed alcohol was an apostate. More dangerously, al-Zarqawi viewed all Shiites as apostates. Under Islamic law, an apostate can be severely punished—even killed. Al-Zarqawi, by declaring Shiites apostates, had thus declared war on a huge portion of Iraq's Muslim population. Al-Zarqawi's army of suicide bombers ravaged Shiite marketplaces, holy shrines, and neighborhoods throughout Iraq.

On August 29, 2003, Mohammad Baqir al-Hakim, a high-ranking Shiite cleric (religious leader), was in the Iraqi city of Najaf to speak at a Shiite shrine. His sermon finished, he walked back to his motorcade. A powerful car bomb detonated and then another. Dozens died in the blasts while the survivors, who had packed the shrine to hear the cleric, panicked and fled. The only part of the cleric recovered was a hand.

News of the attack brought fury in Baghdad, where Shiite crowds marched through the streets in protest. The new Iraq had devolved into an insurgency against the Americans. But it had also become a vicious war between Shiites and Sunnis.

Al-Zarqawi's men began conducting a simple, brutal strategy in cities across Iraq. They would occupy and fortify an abandoned house in a Sunni neighborhood. Then, in a terror campaign, they would scout nearby Shiite areas in groups of three or four, riding in cars, vans, orange-and-white taxis, or BMW sedans with the windows tinted black. David Kilcullen, an Australian counterterrorism expert who served in Iraq with US forces, remembers, "They would kidnap young [Shiite] boys, torture them to death and dump their bodies— eyes gouged out, little limbs and genitals hacked off, cigarette and blowtorch burns all over them (an AQI trademark), the tops of their heads sliced open and electric drills thrust into their brains—back on the streets in front of their houses."

DIVISIONS DEEPEN

In response, Shiite police and militias (informal military units) set up checkpoints in Baghdad. Although most Sunnis and Shiites dress and talk alike, last names, religious mementos, and certain styles of clothing can give away a person's sect. Identifying Sunnis at checkpoints, Shiite militias pulled them aside and shot them. Members of both groups were forced to flee their homes as city populations sorted themselves into exclusive ghettos, where members of the other group wouldn't dare enter.

Nouri al-Maliki, a Shiite, led the new Iraqi government. He became more and more anti-Sunni in his rule. For example, Shiite officials cut off electric power to Sunni sections in Baghdad. While Shiites had electricity throughout the day, Sunni areas were lucky to get four hours. Sewage and water systems run on electricity, so Sunni neighborhoods had no

Osama bin Laden, the founder of al-Qaeda and the mastermind of the 9/11 attacks on the United States, disapproved of al-Zarqawi's war on Shiites in Iraq. He thought jihadists should focus on fighting Americans and other non-Muslim enemies.

running water or flushing toilets when the power was off. Shiites bombed Sunni banks or shut them down, so most Sunnis kept their money at home. This left them vulnerable to robberies. Sometimes Shiites would search Sunni apartments, confiscate hidden money, and then accuse the owners of hoarding the money to support the insurgency then raging across Sunni-dominated areas of Iraq. Any hope of reconciliation with Iraq's Sunni population was quashed.

Al-Qaeda founder Osama bin Laden, in hiding in Pakistan, was appalled by al-Zarqawi's tactics. A Sunni, bin Laden had little concern for Shiites. But he thought AQI's energy would be

WORTH PINKHAM
MEMORIAL LIBRARY
91 Warren Avenue
Ho-Ho-Kus, NJ 07423

better directed in fighting the Americans, not other Muslims. He got his message to al-Zarqawi, who ignored the guidance.

With the escalation of violence in Iraq, many Westerners were beginning to assume that most Muslims—and Islam itself—supported terrorism. To refute the notion, in November 2004, a group of Muslim scholars released a document called the Amman Message. It affirmed Islam's "core values of compassion, mutual respect, tolerance, acceptance, and freedom of religion." It rejected terrorism. And in a direct nod to al-Zarqawi, it rejected his broad understanding of apostasy.

By then, however, al-Zarqawi had taken his campaign further. In May 2004, al-Zarqawi's men had beheaded Nicholas Berg, a captured young American in Iraq. In a video circulated after the killing, five men wearing black hoods push Berg to the floor. As he screams, one of the men puts a knife to his throat. The next shot was Berg's decapitated head on display for the camera.

Al-Zarqawi read a statement in the video. He said, "Hard days are coming to you [Americans]. You and your soldiers are going to regret the day that you stepped foot in Iraq and dared to violate the Muslims. . . . You will see nothing from us except corpse after corpse and casket after casket of those slaughtered in this fashion."

The beheading and the video killed any hope in the United States for a peaceful, stable Iraq. And the United States had a new target: al-Zarqawi.

THE TIDE TURNS

Learning from the fiasco of the first years of occupation, US intelligence officers began to track nearly every phone call, e-mail, and text message moving through Iraq. When a number or address matched information in a US terrorist database, intelligence teams would track the caller's location. Cameras mounted on drones (unpiloted, remotely controlled military aircraft) would bring the target under direct surveillance. Each night elite US Army Delta Force and US Navy SEALs teams climbed into helicopters to capture—or kill—suspects. The US commandos worked with trained military attack dogs. Locals spread the story that "ninjas with lions" were striking Iraqi villages after sundown.

On June 7, 2006, about two years after the Berg murder, al-Zarqawi met with his spiritual adviser in a house north of Baghdad. Unknown to him, a US drone had tracked the adviser and was hovering high over the house. A camera attached to the drone took photographs and sent them to US troops on the ground. In one photo, US intelligence officers saw a grainy image of al-Zarqawi. An F-16 fighter swooped in and dropped two bombs on the house. Minutes later, a group of US soldiers pulled al-Zarqawi's body from the rubble.

Raids such as this, combined with thousands of fresh US troops and a local Sunni revolt against al-Zarqawi's brutality, significantly weakened the insurgency. US military deaths decreased as a result. From 2007 to 2008, the number of US soldiers killed in Iraq fell from 904 to 314. In that time, killings of Iraqi civilians by suicide bombers declined from 3,900 to fewer than 1,700.

By January 2009, a sense of precarious normalcy had come back to the country. AQI, by then called the Islamic State in Iraq, had been driven underground. In April 2010, US and Iraqi forces aimed a volley of rockets and missiles at a hideout in the Iraqi desert just outside Tikrit, where a meeting of the Islamic State's senior leadership was under way. The compound disappeared in a cloud of smoke, killing two leaders who had taken over for al-Zarqawi. The organization soon named a new head: Abu Bakr al-Baghdadi, a scholar of Islamic law.

REBUILDING THE MISSION

Al-Baghdadi was the son of a Sunni imam (leader of worship services) and a member of a tribe that claimed lineage back to Muhammad. He had closely studied the Quran and how its laws are applied to both spiritual questions and the routines of everyday life. When US forces had first invaded Iraq in 2003, al-Baghdadi had joined a resistance group fighting the Americans. US troops captured him along with other insurgents in January 2004.

They sent him to Camp Bucca, a notorious US military prison in the sweltering desert of southern Iraq. There, where daytime temperatures soared well above 100°F (38°C), thousands of prisoners were crammed into tents. To keep the peace, the US guards divided the prisoners by sect, Sunni versus Shiite, housing them in different areas. The most religiously strict Sunnis separated themselves from more moderate Sunnis. Among the religious Sunnis, al-Baghdadi became a leader. He was soon leading thousands of men in daily prayers. The prisoners under al-Baghdadi formed tight bonds and a growing, shared mission of jihadism. Outside observers gave Camp Bucca a nickname: Jihadi University.

The prisoners under al-Baghdadi formed tight bonds and a growing, shared mission of jihadism. Outside observers gave Camp Bucca a nickname: Jihadi University.

When al-Baghdadi was released from the prison ten months later, he joined al-Zarqawi's insurgency. He became a member of a council that discussed and provided guidance on matters of sharia law. For much of the twentieth century, Western nations had dominated the Middle East, both politically and economically. Resentful of Western power, al-Baghdadi predicted that Muslims would one day reestablish a strong empire, as they had had in earlier centuries. "Soon, by Allah's permission, a day will come when Muslims will walk everywhere as a master, having honor, being revered, with his head raised high, and his dignity preserved," al-Baghdadi said in a sermon. "Anyone who dares to offend him will be disciplined, and any hand that reaches out to harm him will be cut off."

By then US forces, helped by moderate Sunni tribes, were stamping out the insurgency. Al-Baghdadi knew that to defeat Western forces and to achieve his grand goal, the Islamic State would have to rebuild itself and its mission. He began looking for a sanctuary, which he spotted in the chaos enveloping a neighboring country—Syria.

3

FROM
INSURGENCY
TO CALIPHATE

n December 17, 2010, a young fruit salesman set himself aflame on the streets of Sidi Bouzid, Tunisia. Through his suicidal act, he expressed his frustration with government corruption and police brutality. The young man's death unleashed the repressed fury of many people across the Muslim world at failed economic policies, repressive dictators, and ineffective government. Within months, the unrest had spread from Tunisia through North Africa and the Middle East. Citizens united to overthrow repressive governments in Tunisia, Libya, Egypt, and Yemen. Observers called the widespread movement the Arab Spring.

Demonstrators denounce Bashar Assad's brutal dictatorship in Syria in December 2011. Assad responded to widespread protests by arresting, torturing, and killing demonstrators and by bombing rebel strongholds inside Syria. Some rebel groups teamed up with ISIS, believing that such a partnership would help them defeat Assad.

At first, the unrest did not spread to Syria and its brutal and dictatorial president, Bashar Assad. In March 2011, however, Syrian police tortured local teens in Daraa, Syria, for writing antigovernment graffiti. In response, angry mobs torched government buildings. Police opened fire on the protesters, killing several. Demonstrations broke out in Syria's largest cities, with protesters calling for Assad's removal.

As protests continued, Assad did not hesitate to use the fist of his security state to maintain power. His forces shot down protesters and manhandled hundreds more into prison. There, guards beat the detainees with clubs, whips, and cables and shocked them with electric current.

In the fall of 2011, most Western security experts believed that Assad's government would fall in a matter of months— maybe weeks. The uprisings were growing, and Syrian army units were defecting to the rebels en masse.

Yet Assad had certain advantages. Some troops were still loyal to him, and they held Syria's biggest cities and ports on the Mediterranean Sea. He could also rely on support from two powerful allies: Iran and Russia. Iran and Syria, both controlled by Shiite leaders, had strong ties to each other, and Syria was the site of Russia's only naval base outside its own borders. The rebel groups fighting Assad were a patchwork of individuals with conflicting goals and methods. These groups appealed for US military aid. Unhappy with Assad's human rights abuses and terrorist connections, the United States considered the request. Analysts in Washington, DC, debated which opposition groups could be trusted with weapons.

By then the United States, led by President Barack Obama, had pulled its troops out of Iraq and Afghanistan. Obama had little appetite for another military incursion in the Middle East. Neither did the American public.

As the world watched, a human rights catastrophe unfolded in Syria. The protests turned into a civil war that became more and more vicious. Assad commanded his air force to drop bombs on Syrian cities, slaughtering civilians and rebels alike. As in Iraq, the society began to split along Sunni and Shiite lines.

ISIS MOVES IN

The chaos in Syria was a perfect opportunity for ISIS to expand its reach and infiltrate the rebel groups with a lethal mixture of violence and bribes.

For example, it targeted Hassan Aboud, the leader of a Syrian rebel group called the Dawood Brigade. The brigade had earned a reputation for discipline and fighting prowess. By 2012 its hundreds of fighters had captured a considerable haul of Syrian army equipment, including nine tanks. But Aboud felt that other Syrian rebel groups gave him too little credit and power. ISIS, seeing his discontent, offered him $2 million, along with weapons and food for his troops, to join its ranks. Aboud agreed. "With money and promises," said a witness, "ISIS got control of hearts and minds" in Syria.

Al-Qaeda had been pushing its ideology in Syria since 2011, but as the war there deepened, relations between ISIS and al-Qaeda deteriorated. Al-Qaeda focused its energy on non-Islamic enemies, and its leaders sharply criticized

Civilians flee through the rubble of Aleppo, Syria, with their belongings. To destroy rebel groups within his nation, President Bashar Assad bombed Aleppo and other Syrian cities. Exploiting the chaos, ISIS moved in to take over large amounts of Syrian territory.

ISIS for its brutal tactics against Muslims. And in April 2013, al-Baghdadi took a step that guaranteed a formal rupture between the two groups. Without informing or consulting with al-Qaeda's leadership, he declared the al-Qaeda organization in Syria to be a part of the Islamic State. Furious, al-Qaeda's leaders issued a public statement of separation from ISIS.

With this split, ISIS moved to become the dominant terrorist group throughout the Middle East. It focused on Iraq, where in December 2012, the Sunni population protested against the Shiite-dominated government in Baghdad. The demonstrators, who were mostly peaceful, built camps and occupied highways. Like many Arab Spring protesters, they asked for less government corruption, more government investment in roads and other infrastructure, and more jobs. In April 2013, Iraqi security units responded to the peaceful protests with force, firing on a crowd in the town of Hawija and killing fifty. As a result, the protests turned violent, and ISIS exploited the chaos. "Sunnis of Iraq," said an ISIS spokesman, "a year ago you began peaceful protests. We warned you then that the nonviolent tactics wouldn't work with the [Shiites]. We told you that they would force you to fight and that is what has now happened. In spite of all the scholars and clerics inside and outside Iraq who told you to avoid violence, now you have picked up weapons against your will."

As Sunnis turned to ISIS for protection, its strength grew in Sunni strongholds across western Iraq, which borders Syria. With the US military gone, ISIS filled the power vacuum and began battling Iraqi security forces. With a power base on the Iraq-Syria border, ISIS looted equipment from both the Iraqi and Syrian armies. Syrian army defectors also joined its ranks.

When Iraqi Shiite security forces continued to crack down on Sunni antigovernment protests, more Sunnis sought out ISIS for protection. Though many Sunnis opposed the group's extremist positions and brutal tactics, they did not trust the Shiites running the government in Baghdad and running the Iraqi army. ISIS was their only option.

"THE JAYVEE TEAM"

In 2014 ISIS advanced into central and northern Iraq. On June 6, ISIS suicide bombers drove jeeps full of explosives into downtown Mosul, Iraq's second-largest city. The slap of explosions, followed by fireballs and angry black smoke, broke over the city skyline. ISIS fighters in pickup trucks raked Iraqi

NOWHERE TO RUN

Of all the groups ISIS targets, Sunnis are caught in the most vicious of traps. ISIS claims to be fighting for the Sunnis, but many Sunnis reject ISIS's intolerance and violence. Other Sunnis remain loyal to the Iraqi state and serve in the police and military. Some, disgusted by al-Zarqawi's savagery, worked with the Americans during the Iraq War.

When ISIS overruns Sunni territory, it moves quickly to find those who have collaborated with the Iraqi government. They are considered traitors. In some towns, ISIS announces that former police and soldiers have twenty-four hours to flee—and they must leave their families behind. ISIS shoots to death those who choose not to leave. It also attacks any local sheikhs who have worked with the Iraqi government, killing them or blowing up their houses.

But Sunnis who flee ISIS often have nowhere to run. If they move to areas controlled by the Shiite-run Iraqi government, they are met with hostility and sometimes violence. Falah Sabar, a forty-eight-year-old Sunni from Anbar, had worked for the Iraqi police. His family fled to Baghdad when ISIS took over his town. It quickly became clear that they were not welcome in the nation's capital. One night a young man knocked on the family's door. Sabar's son answered it. "We don't want you here," the man said. "Your family should be gone by noon tomorrow."

Taking the warning seriously, the family packed up their belongings. But before they had time to flee, more men broke into the home. "You are from Anbar. You are ISIS. You are terrorists," the men charged. The men executed seven of Sabar's family members—brothers, sons, and nephews. Shot in the neck, Sabar was the sole survivor of the massacre.

army defensive lines with machine-gun fire while cells of ISIS fighters rose up within the city. Later that afternoon, a water truck packed with explosives slammed into the Mosul hotel, where many Iraqi senior military commanders were based. The bombs detonated, incinerating the structure.

Terrified, Iraqi forces threw away their equipment and uniforms and fled their posts. In some Sunni-dominated neighborhoods, crowds greeted ISIS fighters as liberators, holding cell phones and cameras aloft to photograph them. The ISIS black flag appeared in house windows and storefronts. The crowds chanted, "We sacrifice our lives and blood for Iraq!"

With their guerrilla tactics, fewer than one thousand ISIS fighters had taken possession of a city of 1.8 million inhabitants. The haul was extraordinary. ISIS seized more than twenty-three hundred US-made Humvees from the Iraqi military, along with caches of arms and ammunition.

ISIS fighters lined up hundreds of captured Shiite Iraqi soldiers, marched them out of the city, and forced them into trucks. The trucks drove to an unknown location, where ISIS videos recorded what happened next. Shiite soldiers—standing in a line or lying down in groups—curse the government in Baghdad for abandoning them. The crack of automatic rifle fire is audible as ISIS fighters stroll among the prisoners, methodically shooting each in the back of the head.

One soldier who survived told of the horror. "One. Two. Three. I was fourth," Ali Hussein Kadhim recalled. "As I turned, I saw the first [soldier] shot in the head. The blood shot up. I thought that was the end for me. There was nothing more to fear. But then I remembered my family."

Who will care for them? Kadhim thought. What will happen to them?

Riding in a truck captured from Iraqi security forces, ISIS fighters cheer as they ride through the streets of Mosul in June 2014. With bombings and machine-gun attacks, ISIS overwhelmed Iraqi army troops there and went on to capture and execute hundreds of Iraqi soldiers.

"He shot the first, the second, the third [soldiers]. Then he came to me. I swear he fired. But I don't know where the bullet went. The guy on one side fell. The guy on the other side fell. There was blood on me. I fell too."

Kadhim lay silently, with blood over his mouth and flies crawling across his face. He dared a glimpse of the executioner's shoe. Hours later, under the cover of darkness, Kadhim fled. Over the next several days, he crossed through ISIS territory, often helped by Sunnis who took pity on him. Three weeks later, he was reunited with his family in southern Iraq.

Shiites in Baghdad felt a palpable unease. ISIS was brutal and merciless—and effective. After losing Mosul, Iraqi forces counterattacked and held the line just hours from the capital city of Baghdad. But ISIS's power was clear.

Western observers were stunned. Told by an adviser that ISIS was only a "flash in the pan," Obama had publicly downplayed the group's strength, referring to them as a junior varsity sports team. "If a J.V. team puts on Lakers uniforms, that doesn't make them Kobe Bryant," Obama said.

ISIS, the "jayvee" team, now controlled a swath of territory stretching from Syria across northern Iraq, home to as many as eight million people. It took in vast amounts of money using several methods. In the territories it conquered, it charged Muslim citizens "taxes," which really meant that it took their money by force. It levied additional taxes on Christians and other non-Muslims living in these territories. Those who refused to pay were executed. Anyone who wanted to travel through or conduct business in ISIS territory had to pay a tax. Another source of revenue was ransom money. The group systematically abducted hundreds of people and requested ransom money from their families for their safe release. Such kidnappings earned ISIS at least $20 million in 2014 alone. Other money came from oil pumped from captured wells and refineries and from looted antiquities sold on the black market.

"CARETAKER TO THE MUSLIM PEOPLE"

On July 4, 2014, Abu Bakr al-Baghdadi entered Mosul's Great Mosque of al-Nuri. He walked to the front of the packed mosque and prepared to climb stairs to the *minbar,* a platform from which he would address the congregation. His every movement was calculated to evoke Muhammad. He paused at each step, as the prophet reportedly had done while climbing a minbar in the seventh century. At the top, he cleaned his mouth with a *miswak,* a small carved stick used by Muslims like a toothbrush. Muhammad had reportedly told followers to use it regularly as a purification of the mouth.

Al-Baghdadi's gestures were based on centuries of Muslim history and culture. In Muhammad's time, the role of leaders among desert-dwelling Arab tribes was critical. Caravans, traveling with their animals to find water and fresh pastureland, could easily get lost in the desert wastes of Arabia, and it was essential that everyone stay together to survive. Leaders had to help their tribes avoid enemies and thieves and to find vital water holes in the vast and dry desert. Muhammad's successors became those leaders, known as *khalif*, the Arabic word for "deputy."

Standing on the ornately carved platform in the Mosul mosque, al-Baghdadi turned to the audience and spoke. He pointed to the many struggles of jihadists to achieve what ISIS had done to that point. Now, it was the obligation of Muslims to declare a caliphate, he said. "This is a duty upon the Muslims—a duty that has been lost for centuries. . . . The Muslims sin by losing it, and they must always seek to establish it."

Islamic caliphates ruled for many centuries over territories ranging at times from Iran to Spain. The last caliphate was the Ottoman Empire, which ruled over Turkey and much of the modern Middle East from the sixteenth to the early twentieth centuries. Al-Baghdadi wanted to restore the caliphate. He claimed his role as the caliph—or successor to Muhammad—as a "heavy responsibility" that made him "caretaker" to the Muslim people. "And I am not better than you," he told them. He promised "a state where the Arab and non-Arab, the white man and black man, the easterner and the westerner are all brothers." This state would be under Islamic rule. "The Earth is Allah's," al-Baghdadi said.

AL-BAGHDADI: THE GHOST

ISIS's leaders are extremely secretive because they understand they are targeted for assassination, drone strikes, and lethal covert operations. Abu Bakr al-Baghdadi rarely appears publicly or in videos. Western intelligence and even al-Baghdadi's own fighters have so little information about him that they refer to him as the Ghost.

"Prepare your arms and supply yourselves with piety [religious feeling]," he continued. "Persevere in reciting the [Quran] with comprehension of its meanings and practice of its teachings. This is my advice to you. If you hold to it, you will . . . own the world."

The caliphate reactivated centuries of Islamic jurisprudence, or bodies of law. According to this law, Muslims are obligated to move to caliphate territory and to join the pure community of believers. If they do not, they are viewed as apostates, especially if they choose to live in regions dominated by other religions. In the new caliphate, captives and members of other religions would all be treated according to ISIS's strict interpretation of Islamic law. This law, according to ISIS, allowed for execution, enslavement, and brutal punishments.

SLAVES OF ISIS

One group that ISIS views as apostates is the Yazidi. This tribe in northern Iraq practices a religion that combines elements of Islam, Christianity, and other faiths. ISIS considers the Yazidi to be infidels. It overran Yazidi territory in August 2014.

Many Yazidis had warning that ISIS was coming—frantic phone calls from neighboring villages and text messages from people who had already fled. Fifty thousand Yazidis sought safety in nearby mountains, especially on sacred Mount Sinjar. They lived there in makeshift shelters made of old blankets, carpets, and scraps of wood and metal.

For some Yazidis, however, the warnings came too late. Layan, a twenty-four-year-old woman, first learned about the arrival of ISIS when fighters swarmed into her town. Firing guns into the air, the ISIS fighters moved through the town and ordered residents to gather at the local schoolhouse.

After fleeing from ISIS fighters, Yazidi refugees rest along an Iraqi roadside. More than three hundred thousand Yazidis fled when ISIS jihadists arrived in their villages. In many cases, those who were unable to escape met a horrific fate. ISIS massacred about five thousand Yazidi men and enslaved about seven thousand Yazidi girls and women.

They were instructed to bring all their money, watches, cell phones, and cars. At the school, the fighters stripped the villagers of their belongings. They were told they would be expelled to the northern territory of Kurdistan, a region historically populated by Kurds. The Yazidi women and men were separated, and the men were driven off in cars.

A twelve-year-old boy soon returned from the men's group and found his mother. "ISIS says they will kill them all [the men]," he said. "They told me to come back because I am too young."

The fighters then forced the women into buses. With curtains drawn across the windows, the buses drove from town to town. At each stop, fighters herded the women into giant halls and presented them for sale to ISIS men as slaves.

An ISIS commander looked Layan over and decided to buy her. He already had two wives. When Layan arrived in their home, they treated her cruelly. They commanded her to read the Quran. When Layan explained she was illiterate, they did not believe her and beat her. When Layan wept at night over what had happened to her family, they mocked her. "You can't read the Quran right," they said. "Why do you cry over your infidel family?"

Layan's sorrow soon hardened into anger. "Why did you kill my brothers?" she asked the commander.

"It's God's will," he replied.

Her captors put Layan to work digging a bomb shelter. After three days, she collapsed from exhaustion. The wives kicked her out of the house in disgust. Layan sought help from a cousin who was enslaved at an ISIS household nearby. The two women decided to escape. They fled into the countryside and stumbled upon a flock of sheep and into a small village. Layan knew the villagers were likely Sunni Arabs, who might return her and her cousin to ISIS. But the women were desperate, so they decided to ask for help.

Instead of returning Layan and her cousin to their ISIS captors, the village welcomed the women. "They kissed our foreheads and said, 'You are like our daughters. Stay here, we won't turn you over to ISIS.'" The women remained in the village for thirty-five days, until they could finally locate and rejoin their families.

Other Yazidi women suffered even worse abuse. One fighter bought a sixteen-year-old girl and kept her locked in a room where the only furniture was a bed. He would enter the room at night to rape her. "She spent the days dreading the smell of the ISIS fighter's breath, the disgusting sounds he made, and pain he inflicted on her body," wrote a *New York Times* reporter.

ISIS follows guidelines on slavery that date back to the time of Muhammad, when Islam allowed the practice. One rule is that a fighter cannot have sex with a slave who is pregnant. ISIS therefore forces slave women to take birth control pills. The pills prevent pregnancy, and different fighters take turns raping each woman. Some Yazidi sex slaves report being raped twenty times daily. If a woman does become pregnant, ISIS forces her to undergo an abortion.

"WE HAVE TO FIGHT"

ISIS massacred five thousand Yazidi men, enslaved seven thousand girls and women, and forced three hundred thousand from their homes. Many of the survivors ended up in refugee camps in northern Iraq and southern Turkey. Others fled by sea, risking their lives in open boats as they tried to reach safety in Europe, across the Mediterranean Sea.

The international community determined that the mass slaughter of the Yazidi men was a genocide—the systematic killing of members of a specific racial, political, religious, or cultural group. After that, no one could doubt that ISIS was more than a jayvee team. Obama ordered air strikes on ISIS forces in Iraq. Other nations, including Canada, the United Kingdom, France, Egypt, and Saudi Arabia, carried out air strikes or contributed troops and equipment to the effort.

Obama was initially reluctant to engage more US troops in Iraq. US support for intervention in Middle Eastern conflicts was at a low point, and he knew that American soldiers would die fighting ISIS. But he also realized the danger of doing nothing. He cited the 2008 Batman movie *The Dark Knight* to explain his decision. "There's a scene in the beginning in which the gang leaders of Gotham are meeting. These are men who had the city divided up. They were thugs, but there was a kind of order. Everyone had his turf. And then the Joker comes in and lights the whole city on fire. . . . [ISIS] has the capacity to set the whole region on fire. That's why we have to fight it."

PRISONERS OF ISIS

By this time, ISIS and its affiliates in Syria had captured several dozen Westerners. They included journalists covering the Syrian civil war and aid workers attempting to provide food, medical care, and other assistance to war-ravaged civilians. Several of the prisoners were women. ISIS knew that these hostages were more valuable alive than dead. A hostage from a wealthy Western nation might be freed in exchange for large amounts of cash or in exchange for the release of jihadists in Western-run prisons. ISIS was therefore willing to negotiate—for the right price. Several European governments paid high ransoms—in some cases, tens of millions of dollars—to win the freedom of hostages from their nations. But the United States and the United Kingdom have laws against paying ransoms to terrorist groups. The rationale is that doing so will only encourage terrorists to take more hostages while enriching their coffers, thereby enabling them to carry out more attacks.

> **"You had to understand that [ISIS] had one objective—to keep us under their thumb. There were no nice guards or good guards—they were all bad."**
>
> **—French journalist Didier François, an ISIS captive**

ISIS treated its hostages with a mixture of cruelty and paranoia. It forced some of them to appear in propaganda videos to threaten and taunt the West. "You had to understand that [ISIS] had one objective—to keep us under their thumb," said Didier François, a French journalist who spent ten months as an ISIS captive. "There were no nice guards or good guards—they were all bad."

One prisoner challenged a guard by looking him in the eye. "I . . . made direct eye contact. Those guards were so sensitive to body language and eye contact. . . . That guard wanted to punch me. . . . He came up to me holding a stick, and he tried to take me down with it, but I stood up. A few minutes later, he came back and he was so angry. He took me away from the jail where I was and beat the crap out of me." Other prisoners endured starvation, waterboarding, extreme cold, and additional tortures.

ISIS was willing to treat a Westerner better if he or she converted to Islam. A number of prisoners did convert, likely under the threat of execution if they didn't. Others, despite reportedly converting, were executed anyway.

Shortly after the US air strikes against ISIS in Iraq began, the group sent a threatening e-mail to the family of one US hostage, journalist James Foley. The message read in part,

> You were given many chances to negotiate the release of your people via cash transactions as other governments have accepted . . . however you proved very quickly to us that this is NOT what you are interested in. . . . Now you return to bomb the Muslims of Iraq once again. . . . Today our swords are unleashed towards you, GOVERNMENT AND CITIZENS ALIKE! AND WE WILL NOT [STOP] UNTILL WE QUENCH OUR THIRST FOR YOUR BLOOD. . . . The first of which being the blood of the American citizen, James Foley.

His head shaved and wearing an orange prison jumpsuit, Foley was beheaded a week later. The execution was captured in a shocking ISIS video distributed online. The killer, wearing a face mask and dressed in black, addressed the camera directly before slicing Foley's throat. "We are an Islamic army and a state that has been accepted by a large number of Muslims worldwide. So, effectively, any aggression toward the Islamic State is an aggression toward Muslims," he said. The executioner spoke in the accented English of someone from North London in England. His real name was Mohammed Emwazi. Born in Kuwait but raised in London, he was one of many Westerners who had traveled to the Middle East to join ISIS. The press nicknamed him Jihadi John.

In the following weeks and months, Jihadi John and other ISIS members executed more captives: Americans, Britons, Frenchmen, Japanese, Egyptians, Syrians—anyone who was taking part in the coalition against ISIS or who appeared to be cooperating with the United States. In several cases, before they were executed, the victims were forced to read statements defending the Islamic State and denouncing the West.

The executions repelled Middle Easterners and Westerners alike. Yet the group's skillful messaging was drawing hundreds of people from around the world into its net.

4

THE KINGDOM
OF GOD

n the summer of 2014, a call from al-Baghdadi echoed
around the world: join us in the caliphate! Over the
next sixteen months, more than thirty Islamic terrorist
groups—from the Middle East, Africa, and Southeast
Asia—pledged allegiance to ISIS.

A Syrian woman was enraptured by al-Baghdadi's
call. "The state of one longing for the caliphate's rule
but physically removed from it is like that of a fish
being hung by its fins over the surface of the sea: it
sees but cannot reach it. The sun burns it with a heat
that sucks the life out of it. Oh Lord, have mercy on
me,"she wrote.

The capital of the new caliphate, the Syrian city
Raqqa (which had also been a caliphate capital between

The ISIS black flag takes its design from an insignia used by Muhammad, the founder of the Islamic religion, in the seventh century. By copying the design, ISIS means to show that it is carrying on Muhammad's legacy.

CE 796 and 809), became a destination for a flood of recruits. "These guys started coming in from all around the world," recalled a Raqqa resident. "It was like New York! A second New York! People from Australia! From Belgium! From Germany! From France! A global tide!"

A twenty-nine-year-old construction worker returned to Raqqa after spending a year in Turkey. He visited a mosque, where the ISIS-affiliated imam spoke passionately about the life of Muhammad and the importance of justice for Muslims. This was far different from the bland, Syrian government–sponsored sermons the man was used to from the days before ISIS arrived. "The hairs on my arms stood up," he recalled. The difference was like "earth and sky."

"THEY SPREAD PANIC"

Residents in Raqqa and other ISIS-controlled towns reported that the jihadists could be polite and courteous—as "sweet as honey," recalled one woman. But such good manners were calculated to win over local populations. Soon residents learned how ISIS truly intended to rule. "They started cutting heads off [and conducting] crucifixions," recalled a witness. "They spread panic everywhere."

Wherever it took over, ISIS enforced a strict interpretation of sharia law. It banned all smoking and drinking. Women had to wear burkas and black shoes. They couldn't wear makeup,

BLACK FLAGS

The most potent symbol of ISIS is its black flag. On the flag, the Arabic script in white reads "No God but God." In black type within a white circle is the message, "Muhammad Is the Messenger of God." ISIS reportedly took the flag's design from an insignia found on a set of letters written by the prophet Muhammad. In earlier eras, writers and government officials often sealed documents using wax or hot metal, which they then stamped with an insignia. A document sealed with a leader's official mark proved that it was authentic. By using the design from Muhammad's insignia, ISIS is sending the message that "the Islamic State had inherited the prophet's seal," said scholar William McCants, "just as the early caliphs had."

and a single woman could not venture in public without a male or older woman as her escort. ISIS issued pamphlets reinforcing the idea that men had complete control over their wives and female relatives. One ISIS pamphlet instructed men how to beat a woman with a "corrective and educational intent." Some women—members of ISIS's all-female al-Khansaa Brigade—had the job of keeping other women in line. They patrolled the streets and accosted any female who was not properly attired or who was walking alone. "They take sticks and strike them on the street if the veil shows the eyes," said a Raqqa resident.

Living under ISIS sometimes resulted in horrific compromises. Many families agreed to marry their daughters to ISIS fighters, fearful of violent punishment if they refused. One Raqqa doctor felt he had no choice but to join the group. "They told me 'if you want to work, you have to join us.' I couldn't live otherwise."

In Raqqa and elsewhere, ISIS closed schools, so many children simply played in the streets during the day. ISIS recruited many preteens and teenagers to join its ranks. It sent them to training camps, where they learned about sharia law and also learned to shoot and make bombs. "At their graduation [the children] have orders to execute someone. Sometimes a beheading, sometimes they just cut off the head of a sheep," said a Raqqa resident.

ISIS skillfully promoted its message through online videos and tweets. Its leaders were well aware that the more gruesome the images, the more people would look. And the more gruesome the images, the more fear would be struck in the hearts of would-be resisters. ISIS became increasingly sadistic. In conquered territories, jihadists sometimes cut out the hearts of rape victims and laid them on their chests. They lined up weeping prisoners before open graves and shot them. They hurled perceived homosexuals to their deaths off high buildings. In videos, jihadist children grinned over severed heads.

Most groups that practice such atrocities try to cover them up. But ISIS bragged about them. After an Iraqi security official reported that ISIS had murdered eight hundred Shiite army cadets, an ISIS spokesperson cheerfully corrected the official—the number had been far higher, he boasted.

A FRESH RECRUIT

Not all ISIS propaganda was gruesome, however. ISIS leaders developed a masterful recruiting campaign, attracting new jihadists with offers of excellent pay, housing, and health care. In a region afflicted by widespread poverty, such offers were extremely enticing. Wakaz Hassan, a nineteen-year-old Iraqi construction worker, had seen online videos of triumphant

An ISIS fighter stands guard at a checkpoint in Mosul in 2014. ISIS pays jihadists well and provides them with housing and other benefits. Joining the terrorist organization can be appealing to those with few economic opportunities.

ISIS soldiers atop a caravan of brand-new Toyota Land Cruisers. The black ISIS flag snapped in the breeze as the conquering jihadists swarmed over fields and into Iraqi towns. Hassan joined ISIS, he said, because his brother had joined and because the group offered to pay him $400 a month, an astronomical sum compared to what he could earn at construction jobs. Hassan signed up for a one-year term.

He underwent military training and was dispatched to Mosul, which had just been captured by ISIS. He soon learned new skills. His commander ordered him to a field, where another ISIS fighter held a blindfolded civilian. The man was crying. The ISIS fighter pushed him to his knees, and the commander handed Hassan a pistol. "They showed me how to do it," Hassan recalled. "You point the gun downward. Also to not shoot directly at the center of the head, but to go a little bit off to one side." Hassan executed the man.

"WHERE TO GO"

To help fighters like Hassan reach its bases in Syria, in 2015 ISIS released a fifty-page e-book called *Hijrah* [pilgrimage] *to the Islamic State*. It describes in detail how to travel to Turkey, which shares a long and largely uncontrolled border with Syria. Like a vacation brochure, the document includes advice on "What to Pack Up. Who to Contact. Where to Go." The book advises recruits to take a number of precautions. It says to keep travel plans secret from everyone, including family. It also cautions recruits to use encryption (message encoding) when communicating online. It notes that Android phones are more secure than iPhones.

Those traveling by plane, the book says, should buy round-trip tickets to and from Turkey. That way, they will look like tourists. It advises them to learn about Turkish tourist attractions and to be "chill to the airport officers," because, after all, "you're just tourists." Any traveler coming directly from the Middle East is a red flag to Turkish police, so the brochure instructs Middle Eastern recruits to fly first to Spain or Greece and then to make their way by car or boat to Turkey. It also tells them how to reach out to ISIS facilitators in Turkey, providing the Twitter accounts of ISIS handlers who can smuggle them across the border.

The brochure promises that once recruits have reached an ISIS facility in Syria, they won't have to pay for housing, electricity, or water. They will receive a monthly tax-free allowance and free medical care. The document warns that life with ISIS won't be comfortable or easy. Since the supply of electrical power is inconsistent in Syria, recruits are instructed to bring a solar battery charger and a headlamp for seeing in the dark. Syrian winters are cold, the brochure notes, so recruits need to bring a warm jacket, hat, and sleeping bag.

"SOUNDS GREAT, RIGHT?"

A main goal of ISIS propaganda is to make the organization look normal. One ISIS video depicts children smiling and waving on an amusement park ride. The group regularly publishes *Dabiq,* an online magazine that puts a positive spin on life under ISIS rule. For example, one issue noted that ISIS provides street cleaning, electrical repairs, nursing care for the elderly, and children's cancer centers in the areas it controls. "The gore and the violence get most of the attention [from the outside world], but that's actually . . . one of the smallest segments of ISIL's over-all messaging," says Brett McGurk of the Global Coalition to Counter ISIL, part of the US State Department. "The majority of their messages are sun-drenched scenes of children eating ice-cream cones and of families—the idealized, utopian vision, which is totally a lie."

In videos, ISIS fighters speak of their contentment. "I don't have the words to express myself about the happiness to be here," says a South African man in one film. Other videos close with welcoming messages: "I wish you were here!" and "Yes, we have created an Islamic utopia here on earth, and you should be part of it." Foreigners shouldn't worry, the videos stress. "You can still survive here even if you don't speak Arabic," says one fighter. "You can find almost every race and nationality here."

Most ISIS recruits are between the ages of sixteen and twenty-five. Once they've arrived, they shed their blue jeans and other Western-style clothes and don traditional long, flowing robes. They become immersed in a world that one Westerner described as filled with "art and emotions."

When they are not in combat, jihadists spend many days relaxing, telling stories, watching movies, and cooking. They are affectionate and even playful with one another. "Jihadist life is emotionally intense, filled with . . . the joy of camaraderie and the elation of religious experience," writes Thomas Hegghammer, director of terrorism research at the Norwegian Defence Research Establishment.

ISIS forbids the playing of musical instruments, so jihadists sing a cappella (voice-only) hymns known as *anashid,* which date from pre-Islamic times. They write their own songs and sing them together in their dorms, in training, and on the battlefield. Poets—both men and women—are greatly respected. Ahlam al-Nasr is a Syrian ISIS recruit in her twenties. Like many other recruits, she chose a new name when she joined ISIS. Her adopted name means "Dreams of Victory." In one of her poems, al-Nasr wrote, "Strike down every adversity, and go reap those heads."

Some recruiting pitches are targeted specifically to the women. A young Scottish convert named Aqsa Mahmood reaches out to female recruits via a blog. She explains that single women must marry ISIS fighters when they arrive; a husband will be chosen for them. Mahmood also notes

> **"The majority of [ISIS] messages are sun-drenched scenes of children eating ice-cream cones and of families—the idealized, utopian vision, which is totally a lie."**
>
> —Brett McGurk,
> Global Coalition to Counter ISIL

that ISIS does not allow women to fight on the front lines. But their role in jihad—caring for their husbands and having children—is just as vital, she says. After all, "Who will raise the next generation of Lions?"

Mahmood also brags on her blog about the loot—ovens, refrigerators, even milk shake makers—that ISIS fighters have stolen from terrorized populations. "There is something so pleasurable to know that what you have taken from the Kuffar [unbeliever] [has been] handed to you personally by Allah as a gift." She also promises "a house with free electricity and water provided to you due to the Khilafah [caliphate], and no rent included. Sounds great, right?"

A HARSH REALITY

Once in Syria, a thirty-eight-year-old Jordanian recruit, Abu Ali, was astonished at the variety of people who had come to join ISIS. His group of fellow recruits reminded him of an international airport, with Americans, Britons, and French among the crowd. An emir, or local Muslim leader, moved among the recruits, smiling and encouraging them. Ali was struck by how welcoming the ISIS men were and how easily they made promises.

"I don't want to fight, just an administration job," Ali told them.

"No problem," the emir answered. But he clarified that Ali, like all recruits, would have to complete a religious course and military training. Ali traveled with dozens of other recruits to a mountain camp, where they received religious instruction. The day started at dawn with prayer, followed by physical activity—jogging and push-ups. Breakfast was stale bread and cubes of cheese washed down with water. Lectures on religion filled the next several hours. Teachers stressed the importance of fighting infidels and punishing apostates. Dinner was beans and more bread. Afterward, the recruits listened to announcements or watched video clips of world news.

One night, a video clip showed a man in an orange jumpsuit sitting in a cage. The prisoner was a Jordanian air force pilot who had ejected from his damaged plane during a bombing run on ISIS. He had parachuted into ISIS hands. His captors had then caged him and soaked him in gasoline. The video clip showed jihadists pouring more gasoline around the cage and then setting the liquid on fire.

The flames leaped toward the cage, swarmed beneath the wooden floorboards, and climbed up the pilot's body. The man covered his face with his hands and then put them down again, his face contorting in pain. The fire swallowed the pilot. His blackened figure lurched against the bars and fell to its knees.

The video shocked Ali, but he continued with his training. He learned to load and fire an AK-47 assault rifle. He shot rocket-propelled grenades. Along with other recruits, he ran for long stretches. On the last day of military training, he and the other recruits swore an oath to ISIS.

Despite protesting that he wanted an administrative job, Ali and other raw recruits traveled to a combat zone in Iraq. Their commander, an ex-officer from the Iraqi army, pointed at an earthen berm, or mound, about 0.25 miles (0.4 kilometers) away. The Iraqi army was entrenched there, he said. The ISIS fighters would seize the position the next morning. Ali looked aghast at the open, exposed fields leading up to the berm. "How . . . are we going to capture that berm?" he asked. "It's twelve of us against the Iraqi army!"

"Allah is with you," the officer said. "You will be victorious."

SHOWDOWN AT DABIQ

Many religious writings predict a final battle between good and evil called the apocalypse. In Islam the apocalypse is mainly described in the hadith. This text says that the apocalypse will occur after a period of injustice against Muslims, who will then be united by a caliph. The apocalypse will come, according to the hadith, with a final battle against the enemies of Islam at the Syrian town of Dabiq. The battle will vanquish evil, and an era of peace and righteousness will follow.

In November 2014, ISIS executed American aid worker Peter Kassig at Dabiq. "Here we are, burying the first American Crusader in Dabiq, eagerly waiting for the remainder of your armies to arrive," announced the executioner. But when coalition forces did arrive in Dabiq, in October 2016, the apocalypse did not come. Instead, Dabiq fell to the coalition and both sides continued to fight.

Backed by Turkish and other coalition forces, members of the Free Syrian Army—a militia that opposes both Assad and ISIS—move into Dabiq, Syria, in October 2016. The coalition was successful in retaking the town from ISIS.

A few hours later, another officer offered Ali a suicide belt—a belt packed with explosives. Ali could use it to blow himself up—and at the same time kill many Iraqi soldiers—if his situation was hopeless. According to ISIS's worldview, those who martyr themselves for the cause of jihad will enter paradise, or heaven, after death. "Why don't you wear [the belt]?" Ali snapped at the officer. "You want to go to paradise more than I do."

The ISIS commanders assigned Ali to a medical team. The next morning, the attack went forward in the predawn darkness. Bullets whipped and cracked around Ali as he pulled bloodied, screaming companions from the line of fire. If he couldn't move a wounded man, Ali was supposed to give him a bomb, so he could blow himself up as Iraqi soldiers advanced—killing them and martyring himself.

According to ISIS's worldview, those who martyr themselves for the cause of jihad will enter paradise, or heaven, after death.

The fight raged for three days. Dozens of ISIS fighters were killed, and many were left to die. Ali, exhausted, confronted his commander. "We don't want to fight anymore. You are leaving dead and wounded men behind," he said.

In response, the commander sent Ali to the rear of the unit. His faith in ISIS shattered, Ali eventually escaped to Turkey.

5
LOOKING WEST

By 2015 more than 4,500 Westerners had joined ISIS. The most—more than 1,000—were from France, which has the second-largest Muslim population in Europe. But many came from the United Kingdom (500), Germany (550), and Belgium (500) as well. Another 150 came from the Netherlands, Austria, Denmark, and Canada. One of the most well-known Western recruits was Jihadi John (Mohammed Emwazi), the British executioner seen in many ISIS videos. After earning a graduate degree in computer programming from a British university and working as an information technology salesperson, he joined ISIS in 2012. He died in a US drone strike in 2015.

Another Western recruit was fifteen-year-old Adèle, from Paris. One afternoon in 2012, her mother started to worry when Adèle did not return from school. She found a note in her daughter's room:

Security cameras at Gatwick Airport in London photographed three British schoolgirls in February 2015, before they boarded a plane bound for Turkey. From there they crossed the border into Syria to join ISIS. British news agencies reported that one of the girls died in an air strike on Raqqa, Syria, in 2016.

My own darling Mamaman . . .

It's because I love you that I have gone. When you read these lines I'll be far away. I will be in the Promised Land, the Sham [eastern Mediterranean], in safe hands. Because it's there that I have to die to go to Paradise. . . . I have been chosen and I have been guided. And I know what you do not know; we're all going to die, punished by the wrath of God. It's the end of the world, Mamaman. There is too much misery, too much injustice. . . . And everyone will end up in hell. Except for those who have fought with the last Imam in the Sham, Except for us.

Adèle had left both her computer and her cell phone behind. A search of the computer turned up evidence: photos of Adèle wearing a black niqab (similar to a burka), a record of her online conversion to Islam, and a hidden Facebook account in which she called herself Oum Hawwa, or "Mother of Eve."

Authorities determined that Adèle had joined al-Qaeda in Syria after extensive online conversations with a man calling himself Brother Mustapha. Adèle had been feeling enormous sorrow after a beloved aunt had died, a vulnerability that Mustapha at first treated gently. But as Adèle fell further under Mustapha's influence, the online conversations turned sinister. He wrote, "When I tell you to call me you must call me. I want you pious and submissive to Allah and to me. I can't wait to see your two little eyes beneath the niqab."

One day a text message appeared on Adèle's cell phone. The messenger wrote, "Oum Hawwa died today. She was not chosen by God. She didn't die a martyr: just a stray bullet. May you hope she doesn't go to hell."

Adèle's story is not unique. Another fifteen-year-old French ISIS recruit told her frantic mother in a cell phone conversation from the Middle East, "You should know that I am no longer your daughter. I belong to God. I will never return to the land of the unbelievers. If your government of unbelievers should come to find me with an army, we will execute every last one of them, the Truth will win out, we are afraid of nothing. We love death more than you love life."

> **"You should know that I am no longer your daughter. I belong to God. . . . If your government of unbelievers should come to find me with an army, we will execute every last one of them. . . . We love death more than you love life."**
>
> —ISIS recruit from France, aged fifteen

Yet another recruit was Jejoen Bontinck of Antwerp, Belgium. At the age of sixteen, Jejoen converted to Islam and joined a radical group called Sharia4Belgium. Three years later, in 2013, he packed a suitcase with a sleeping bag, clothes, a flashlight, and night vision goggles. The next day, he was in Syria, living in a walled villa with a unit of about seventy international jihadi recruits.

Life at the villa included weapons training, lectures by Islamic scholars, and sentry duty. The recruits also set up roadblocks on nearby highways. Focusing on buses, they searched through passengers' bags for any evidence that would identify someone as a non-Sunni. They looked for crosses that marked riders as being Christian or cell phone pictures of the Iranian ayatollah (religious leader) that identified a person as being Shiite. The jihadists-in-training confiscated the passengers' belongings, including jewelry, laptop computers, cell phones, and cash. They held some passengers for

Jejoen Bontinck left Belgium to join ISIS but soon wanted out. He escaped and returned to Belgium, where he was arrested for affiliating with terrorists. Because he cooperated with police, providing them with valuable intelligence on ISIS, he did not go to prison.

ransom and killed the hostage if his or her family didn't pay. One Sharia4Belgium member called his girlfriend and bragged about shooting a man in the head.

After three days of such activity, Jejoen had had enough. He asked to return to Belgium, but his trainers would not let him go. They first imprisoned him and then posted him on the front lines, fighting for ISIS north of Aleppo, Syria.

By then Jejoen's father, Dimitri Bontinck, was looking for him in Syria. Eventually father and son connected via text message. The elder Bontinck paid local smugglers to take Jejoen across the Turkish border, where the two were reunited. They flew home to Belgium.

ISIS jihadists use explosives to destroy a temple in Palmyra, Syria, in 2015. The destruction in Palmyra is part of a widespread ISIS effort to wipe out symbols and monuments representing non-Islamic culture.

Jejoen was one of the lucky ones. According to Daniel Koehler, director of the German Institute on Radicalization and De-radicalization Studies, only a small fraction of the Europeans who have joined ISIS in Syria have made it home.

CULTURAL DESTRUCTION

Since 2014 ISIS has looted, bulldozed, or bombed dozens of mosques, shrines, churches, monasteries, museums, libraries, and ancient monuments and buildings in Iraq and Syria. Some of the structures date back thousands of years to the earliest empires in the world. ISIS says that the destruction is justified, since the structures and sites promote non-Islamic religions or, in the case of the mosques and shrines, the Shiite sect of Islam. ISIS sells many of the valuable artifacts and antiquities from the sites on the black market.

In May 2015, ISIS captured the desert city of Palmyra, Syria. Because of its rich cultural and historical treasures, including statues, temples, towers, and castles dating to the first and second centuries CE, the United Nations Educational, Scientific and Cultural Organization (UNESCO) had named it a World Heritage Site. Once part of the Roman Empire, the city was an important trade center linking Rome with Persia, India, and China. ISIS fighters blew up many of the ancient structures there (*left*), since they dated to an era before Islam, which ISIS views as a "time of blackness." The jihadists also beheaded a Syrian archaeologist who oversaw research at the site.

Syrian troops, backed by Western forces, drove ISIS out of Palmyra in March 2016, but in December, ISIS captured the city again. It continued with its destruction, this time smashing a sixteen-columned structure called the Tetrapylon and the facade of a theater. UNESCO has vowed to safeguard and preserve Palmyra, but as long as ISIS is active, this promise will be difficult to keep.

AMERICAN JIHAD

In an ISIS propaganda video released in May 2014, twenty-two-year-old Moner Mohammad Abusalha—a Florida native—tears his US passport apart and sets it aflame. He holds an AK-47 as he describes how easy it was for him to travel from the United States to Turkey and then across the Syrian border to join ISIS.

His life is now complete, he says to the camera. "Just sitting down, five minutes, drinking a cup of tea with mujahideen is better than anything I've experienced in my whole life. I lived in America! I know how it is: you have all the fancy amusement parks, and the restaurants, and the food . . . and you think you're happy. You're not happy. . . . I was always sad and depressed. Life sucked. All you do is work forty, fifty, sixty hours a week."

Abusalha describes the paradise that awaits ISIS martyrs. In heaven, he says, a martyr will encounter a woman so beautiful that "you would die from her beauty."

His eyes welling with tears, he addresses his family in Florida. "I love you mom. I love you bro. Look after our sister and our little brother." The video then shows a truck driving into a Syrian army post. The scene ends with a thunderous explosion. Abusalha had just become ISIS's first American suicide bomber.

Hoda Muthana, a twenty-year-old college student from Birmingham, Alabama, was another American recruit. In 2014 she told her parents that she was going on a school field trip to Atlanta, Georgia. She ended up joining ISIS in Syria, where she took the name Umm Jihad, or "Mother of the Jihad." ISIS married her to an Australian jihadist, who was killed in fighting three weeks later.

Muthana remained in touch with family and friends in the

United States through a Twitter account. She tweeted that her dead husband had achieved his "long-desired martyrdom." She posted photographs of herself and four other female jihadists, each covered in a black niqab and holding an AK-47. They posed atop a white BMW, with the words "Chillin' in the Khalifa [caliphate]" at the bottom of the photo. Twitter finally shut down her account, but before it did, she used it as a tool to recruit more Americans to ISIS. "Sooooo many Aussies [Australians] and Brits [British] here," she tweeted. "But where are the Americans. Wake up u cowards."

LONE WOLVES

Most of the Americans and Europeans who have joined ISIS grew up in Muslim families. Many of them felt like outsiders in Western nations and were drawn to ISIS for a sense of belonging. Ali Amin, a seventeen-year-old son of a Yemeni immigrant family, felt isolated in his Virginia suburb. Curious about ISIS, he surfed the Internet and found ISIS contacts in Great Britain, Finland, and South Africa. Amin started a jihadist-themed Twitter account with the handle @AmreekiWitness. It attracted thousands of followers. A lonely teenager, Amin suddenly had respect, power, and purpose. For the first time," he said, "I felt I was not only taken seriously about very important and weighty topics, but was actually being asked for guidance."

> "Just sitting down, five minutes, drinking a cup of tea with mujahideen is better than anything I've experienced in my whole life."
>
> —Moner Mohammad Abusalha of Florida, an ISIS suicide bomber

Through his tweets, Amin lured the US State Department's anti-Islamic State Twitter account, @ThinkAgainTurnAway, into an exchange. Federal agents eventually arrested Amin and sentenced him to eleven years in prison. He is far from alone. By 2015 US officials had charged more than fifty Americans with the crime of supporting the Islamic State.

Although they desire to join ISIS, not all Western recruits are able to travel thousands of miles—and across the ocean in the case of Americans—to reach Syria. For these would-be jihadists, in the spring of 2015, ISIS published a seventy-one-page electronic document called *How to Survive in the West*. Written in English, it tells ISIS supporters in both Europe and North America how to disguise their ISIS affiliations from friends and family. It offers guidance on how to avoid scrutiny from the authorities. For those with Arabic birth names, the booklet includes tips on adopting Western-sounding nicknames.

ISIS also encourages Western jihadists to carry out lone-wolf attacks. That is, it tells those who can't join with other jihadists how to attack the enemies of ISIS on their own. In online speeches, ISIS spokespeople have urged lone-wolf attackers to kill "citizens of the countries that entered into a coalition against [the] Islamic State. . . . Kill him in any manner or way however it may be."

Many people have responded to this call. Would-be jihadist John T. Booker planned to attack a US Army installation in Kansas. As the moment approached, he shared his feelings on Facebook. "I will soon be leaving you forever, so goodbye! I'm going to wage jihad and hope that I die." He continued, "Getting ready to be killed in jihad is a HUGE adrenaline rush! I am so nervous. NOT because I'm scared to die but eager to meet my Lord." The FBI caught him outside the army base, attempting to detonate a fake bomb supplied to him by an undercover government agent.

Another lone wolf was Syed Rizwan Farook, a twenty-eight-year-old county health inspector in Riverside, California. He had met his wife, Tashfeen Malik of Pakistan, on a Muslim dating website. Both Farook and Malik had pledged allegiance to ISIS on Facebook, even though they had never communicated with the group. On December 2, 2015, the couple entered a holiday party at the office where Farook worked in nearby San Bernardino. He knew everyone there.

A police SWAT team mobilizes to track down two ISIS-inspired terrorists who massacred fourteen county workers and wounded twenty-two others at an office holiday party in San Bernardino, California, in 2015.

The couple emptied four thirty-round magazines (ammunition chambers) into the crowd, killing fourteen and wounding twenty-two. Farook and Malik fled the scene in a black SUV. Police eventually cornered the vehicle and killed them both.

About six months later, a gay nightclub in Orlando, Florida, was the scene of another lone-wolf attack. At about 2 a.m. on June 12, 2016, a crowd at the Pulse nightclub was dancing to the rhythm of Latin reggae. The music was suddenly overwhelmed by a series of loud bangs. Some clubgoers thought the succession of popping sounds was part of the entertainment.

> **"All I heard was a laugh. He laughed . . . an evil laugh, something that's just going to be imprinted in my head forever."**
> **—Norman Casiano, who was shot in the Pulse nightclub by lone-wolf jihadist Omar Mateen**

A single gunman, armed with an AR-15-style assault rifle, was firing steadily into the crowd. The DJ, Simeon Alberto Roman Barria, took cover behind an amplifier and watched the gunman. "I heard him laugh," said Roman. "I heard him change the magazines and throw them down when he was done; it was so fast. He knew what he was doing."

The gunman then walked into the woman's bathroom and began shooting people hiding inside the stalls. Norman Casiano was shot twice in the back. He heard other victims plead for mercy. In reply, "All I heard was a laugh," said Casiano. "He laughed . . . an evil laugh, something that's just going to be imprinted in my head forever."

Police entered the building minutes after the first shots. On the dance floor, Officer Omar Delgado saw huddled forms lying together. "Hey, come on, get up! Let's go!" he shouted.

"We have cover for you. Police! We're here." No one moved—they were dead.

At 2:35, a call came into 911. The gunman was calling from the Pulse bathroom:

DISPATCHER Emergency 911, this is being recorded.

GUNMAN In the name of God the Merciful, the beneficent . . .

DISPATCHER What?

GUNMAN Praise be to God, and prayers as well as peace be upon the prophet of God [Arabic words]. I wanna let you know, I'm in Orlando and I did the shootings.

DISPATCHER What's your name?

GUNMAN My name is I pledge of allegiance to Abu Bakr al-Baghdadi of the Islamic State.

DISPATCHER O.K. What's your name?

GUNMAN I pledge allegiance to Abu Bakr al-Baghdadi may God protect him . . . on behalf of the Islamic State.

DISPATCHER All right, where are you at?

GUNMAN In Orlando.

In the bathroom, terrified hostages watched the gunman methodically wash and dry his hands. At 2:48 he spoke on the phone to a police negotiation team working outside the club. The gunman claimed to be an Islamic soldier fiercely opposed to US air strikes in Syria and Iraq. He threatened the officers with sniper fire and bombs.

The standoff continued until 5:14 a.m., when police broke into the bathroom with an armored vehicle. The gunman died in an exchange of bullets. A search of the club revealed no explosives or suicide vests.

Raul Mata adjusts a photo of his friend Cory James Connell, one of the victims of the 2016 Pulse nightclub shooting, at a makeshift memorial in Orlando. The killer, Omar Mateen, was a lone-wolf jihadist claiming allegiance to the Islamic State.

The gunman was soon identified as twenty-nine-year-old Omar Mateen, born in New York City to Afghani immigrant parents. The FBI had previously investigated him—once for making comments that seemed sympathetic to terrorism to his coworkers and a second time because one of his acquaintances had carried out a suicide bombing in Syria. Authorities thought he had perhaps been involved. The FBI inquiries were inconclusive, however, and Mateen was not arrested or charged. Mateen went on to commit mass murder at Pulse, where he killed fifty people and wounded more than fifty others. It was the deadliest attack on the gay community in American history and the most destructive act of terrorism on US soil since September 11, 2001.

6

THE CHALLENGE
OF OUR TIMES

y the summer of 2015, civil wars were raging in
Syria, Iraq, Libya, and Afghanistan. Government
institutions had broken under the strain. In Syria alone,
more than four million people had fled their homes,
trying to escape both ISIS and Assad's brutal crackdown
against rebel fighters.

Many Syrians crossed into Turkey and crowded into
refugee camps. Their cities destroyed by Assad's bombs
and with no homes to return to, the refugees pushed
westward by the hundreds of thousands. They ventured
onto the Aegean Sea in small boats and makeshift
rafts, heading for sanctuary in Greece. Many of the
vessels capsized in the open water, and hundreds of
people drowned. The survivors packed into trains bound

Syrian and Afghan refugees arrive in Greece after crossing the
Aegean Sea in an open boat. These refugees and thousands more
are fleeing civil war and terrorism in their homelands. Debates
about how to integrate the mostly Muslim refugees into Western
societies are raging across Europe and the United States.

for European cities. They sought normalcy—peace, order,
employment, and hope for the future. Germany agreed to
take in more than one million Syrian refugees. The United
Kingdom set its quota at twenty thousand. The United States
agreed to accept ten thousand.

But despite government efforts to resettle the Syrian
refugees, across Europe and the United States, many citizens
wanted to refuse them entry altogether. Most of the refugees
were Muslims, and many of them observed sharia law. The
anti-immigrant voices said that sharia law was incompatible
with the democratic, secular societies of the West. Some
worried that jihadists would enter their nations along with
the refugees. Several European nations, such as Hungary,
Slovakia, and Poland, closed their borders to Syrian refugees
altogether.

TRIED-AND-TRUE TERRORISM

Back in the Middle East, ISIS began losing territory to well-
organized Iraqi and US-led forces. So it changed its tactics,
reverting to those honed during the insurgency in Iraq. It
increased suicide bombings, from about two per day in 2015
to more than three per day in 2016.

In a single two-week period in March 2016, ISIS killed 247
people in terrorist attacks in six countries—Belgium, Turkey,
Iraq, Nigeria, Ivory Coast, and Pakistan. The victims came

from twenty-six countries. Almost 50 of them were under the age of eighteen, and 17 of them were aged ten or younger. In Pakistan 10 members of the same family were cut down by ISIS. "My son was like a candle in the house," said an Iraqi father whose son died in an ISIS bombing. "This candle was snuffed out, and the happiness of the family is gone."

In mid-2016, ISIS launched an offensive during the holy Islamic month of Ramadan. Suicide bombers and gunmen attacked the international airport in Istanbul, Turkey, killing 44. In Dhaka, Bangladesh, five young men affiliated with ISIS stormed a restaurant and, after separating out Muslims, slaughtered everyone else. In Baghdad, an ISIS car bomb exploded in a packed Shiite shopping district, killing more than 280 people. On the evening of July 14 in Nice, France, a truck barreled into a crowd gathered to watch fireworks. When the truck finally came to a halt, its driver shot dead by police, dozens of mutilated bodies lay in the street. ISIS declared the driver to be a "soldier of the Islamic State" who had "executed the operation in response to calls to target citizens of coalition nations, which fight the Islamic State." In December 2016, another driver repeated the tactic in Berlin, Germany, this time steering a truck through an outdoor market, killing 12. On New Year's Eve in Istanbul, Turkey, a lone gunman entered a nightclub and murdered 39 partygoers in seven minutes of carnage. ISIS took credit for the attack the next day.

In a single two-week period in March 2016, ISIS killed 247 people in terrorist attacks in six countries—Belgium, Turkey, Iraq, Nigeria, Ivory Coast, and Pakistan.

Iraqi soldiers launch missiles at Islamic State fighters in a village south of Mosul in October 2016. By 2017 coalition forces had retaken large swaths of territory previously captured by ISIS.

On the battlefield, however, ISIS was losing ground. By 2017, supported by US airpower and intelligence, Iraqi forces had recaptured significant territory, including the cities of Tikrit and Ramadi. About twenty thousand ISIS fighters had been killed in the campaign. In Syria in January, coalition-backed fighters pushed toward ISIS's capital city, Raqqa. By then the coalition had virtually sealed off the Turkish–Syrian border, making it almost impossible for ISIS to receive goods and recruits from that direction.

And coalition forces were striking ISIS's funding sources. Coalition police tracked down ISIS bank accounts and froze them. American air strikes targeted ISIS-held oil fields, pipelines, and vehicles. Air strikes also incinerated ISIS warehouses filled with millions of dollars of cash. Altogether, ISIS revenue had declined by one-third, and ISIS was forced to cut its fighters' pay in half.

"BOMB THOSE SUCKERS"

President Barack Obama had resisted calls to send US ground troops into Iraq and Syria to fight ISIS. Obama had argued that this was exactly what the terrorists wanted: the United States to be mired in an unwinnable war in the Middle East. Moreover, many political analysts believed that the sight of US soldiers fighting Muslims in the Middle East would be a powerful recruiting tool for ISIS. So Obama and other Western leaders had tried to downplay the threat of ISIS and to resist direct engagement.

US policy quickly changed in January 2017. A new president—Republican Donald Trump, a real estate tycoon and former reality TV star—took office. On the campaign trail, Trump had spoken aggressively about ISIS, threatening to "bomb those suckers [ISIS]." Trump was also a leading voice in a growing anti-immigrant movement in the United States. In his campaign appearances and tweets, he vowed that if he were elected, he would ban Muslim immigration to the United States. He said that barring Muslims would keep the nation safe from terrorism.

THE ETHICS OF DRONE STRIKES

The campaign against ISIS and terrorism has raised difficult moral and ethical questions. For example, US drones *(below)* deliver missile strikes throughout the Middle East to target ISIS fighters and bases. But while killing terrorists, many missions also wound and kill civilians. In July 2016, a White House report claimed that US drone strikes had killed between 64 and 116 civilians in Afghanistan, Syria, and Iraq from 2009 to 2015. The report stated that the same strikes had killed between 2,372 and 2,581 terrorists.

In October 2013, critics of the drone program called for congressional hearings so that US lawmakers could learn about the suffering of drone strike victims. Only five members of Congress attended the hearings. A Pakistani family talked about a drone strike that had killed their mother and grandmother a year earlier. She was gathering okra in a field with her two grandchildren when a missile struck nearby. "She was the string that held our family together," her son told the US lawmakers. "Since her death, the string has been broken and life has not been the same. We feel alone and we feel lost."

The son also said that drone strikes had driven people inside. "Now I prefer cloudy days when the drones don't fly. When the sky brightens and becomes blue, the drones return and so does the fear," he said. "Children don't play so often now, and have stopped going to school."

Supporters of drone strikes say that drones provide an effective way to kill those who would kill Americans. By sending in remotely controlled vehicles, the military doesn't have to put US pilots and other fighters in harm's way. Civilian casualties are regrettable, supporters of drone strikes say, but the solution is to be more careful, not to stop using drone missile strikes. Critics argue for a ban on drone strikes and say that it is always unacceptable for innocent civilians to die in war.

President Donald Trump's pledge to ban Muslim immigration into the United States to thwart terrorism faces stiff opposition. Here, protesters at an interfaith rally in New York City denounce the proposed ban in December 2016. Opponents point out that the US Constitution protects religious freedom and say that a ban based on religion is unconstitutional.

After his inauguration, Trump quickly made good on his promise. In late January, he issued an executive order that temporarily prohibited the entry of immigrants from seven countries with Muslim majorities—Iraq, Iran, Sudan, Somalia, Syria, Libya, and Yemen. The order sparked protests in Boston and New York, as well as an angry march in front of the White House. The US Constitution guarantees freedom of religion, and many Americans saw Trump's order as a direct threat to that freedom. Even leading Republicans seemed to be taken aback by the order. "I think we need to be careful," said Senate majority leader Mitch McConnell. "We don't have religious tests [for citizens and residents] in this country."

Other Americans approved of Trump's order. They were frightened of ISIS and wanted their leaders to take the threat more seriously. "The [terrorists] have a purpose, a religious rationale, and a global network of supporters and enablers. The scale of their project, its ambition, and its limitless cruelty make it far more dangerous than previous terrorist enterprises," wrote columnist Clive Crook on the website Bloomberg.com.

Trump's presidential victory and quick actions against Muslim immigrants emboldened right-wing movements across Europe and the United States. Drawing on a growing fear of terrorism, anti-refugee politicians surged ahead in the polls in Scandinavian countries, the Netherlands, and Germany. In France the National Front, a xenophobic (antiforeigner), ultraconservative party, has long claimed that France is losing its cultural identity to immigrants. National Front leader Marine Le Pen, a French presidential candidate, said that Trump's victory "shows that people are taking their future back." Even if Le Pen, Trump, and others fail in their bids to block Muslim immigration, the undercurrent of fear and rage that they have tapped into will not simply go away.

A WORLD AFTER ISIS?

What lies ahead? Nothing is certain. However, given the deep roots of terrorism and the rage and commitment that fuel it, the killing will likely go on. The US-led coalition will continue military operations to crush ISIS. Security forces in the Middle East, Europe, the United States, and elsewhere will have to remain on guard and anticipate the next terrorist threat.

What will Donald Trump do? He has signaled his intention

SECURITY VERSUS FREEDOM: TRADE-OFFS

In May 2013, Edward Snowden, a former technology contractor for the US National Security Agency (NSA), revealed thousands of documents that showed that the NSA engages in a far-reaching and extensive surveillance operation. It secretly monitors the cell phone usage, e-mail messages, social media accounts, and Internet traffic of millions of Americans and foreigners, including foreign leaders.

Many US citizens say that such surveillance is wrong. They believe that government surveillance violates their right to privacy, which is guaranteed by the US Constitution. But the NSA argues that its surveillance efforts are critical to detecting, monitoring, and defeating terrorist activities. General Keith Alexander, the director of the NSA, told Congress in 2013 that NSA surveillance efforts had thwarted at least fifty terrorist attacks.

Alexander and other NSA officials argue that the NSA must collect vast amounts of data to find a needle in a haystack. The needle, in this case, is a terrorist e-mail, and the haystack is made of the billions of e-mails sent around the world each day. The NSA argues that it must monitor all those messages to uncover individual messages that might be critical for national security.

While many Americans oppose NSA data collection, others agree that it's vital to US security. They say that Americans might have to sacrifice some privacy to stay safe from terrorism. But how much privacy should we trade off for security? That question remains a topic of heated debate.

to work more closely with Russia in the Middle East. He has promised swift, aggressive action against ISIS. Shortly after taking office, he asked the leaders of the US military to submit plans on how to defeat ISIS. Most likely, these recommendations will be similar to what was done during

Police forces and government agencies across the United States have beefed up their counterterrorism efforts in the wake of ISIS attacks. Some criticize the increased surveillance, saying that it threatens US citizens' rights to privacy. Others say the surveillance is critical to keeping Americans safe from terrorism.

the Obama years. Iraqi and other forces will fight ISIS on the ground, supported by US air power, intelligence, weapons, and training. The large question for Trump—and the American people—is whether large numbers of US troops will join the battle on the ground.

For its part, ISIS vows to continue fighting. "Do you think, America, that defeat is by the loss of towns or territory?" asked ISIS spokesman Abu Muhammad al-Adnani in 2016. "Were we defeated when we lost the cities of Iraq and retreated to the desert without a city or a land? No, true defeat is losing the will and desire to fight."

In Turkey a reporter spoke with a man who claimed to be part of the intelligence wing of ISIS. He was there, he said, to set up secret cells of ISIS fighters who would remain hidden in the short term. They would emerge later to carry on the struggle, even if the caliphate were overwhelmed. "Our enemies are clever and determined," he told the reporter. "What we can do is to make sure the body of the state [caliphate] is strong, so that it can heal no matter how far they weaken it. So even if they destroy us in one area, you can be sure we're still there."

> **"Were we defeated when we lost the cities of Iraq and retreated to the desert without a city or a land? No, true defeat is losing the will and desire to fight."**
>
> —ISIS spokesperson Abu Muhammad al-Adnani

In July 2016, James B. Comey, director of the US Federal Bureau of Investigation, agreed with this assessment. He said that even if ISIS were to be crushed in the Middle East, hundreds of radical ISIS warriors would flee to western Europe and potentially to the United States. He compared the situation to the war in Afghanistan in the 1980s and early 1990s. After the Soviet Union withdrew in defeat, hardened foreign-born jihadists returned to their homelands, where they formed terrorist groups and spread havoc. "[ISIS strength] is 10 times that [of the Afghanistan jihadists] or more," Comey warned. The ISIS threat "is an order of magnitude greater than anything we've seen before." Defeating that threat will be the challenge of our times.

SOURCE NOTES

6–7 "Paris Attacks: Eyewitness Accounts," *BBC News,* November 16, 2015, http://www.bbc.com/news/world-europe-34813570.

7 Alexandra Ma, "Horrifying Eyewitness Accounts from Paris Attack Survivors," *Huffington Post,* November 13, 2015, http://www .huffingtonpost.com/entry/paris-attack-survivor-eyewitness -account_us_5646763ae4b0603773492620.

7 Adam Nossiter, "Hostage at Bataclan Recalls Terrorists during Paris Attack," *New York Times,* December 31, 2015, https://www .nytimes.com/2016/01/01/world/europe/bataclan-hostage-paris -terror-attack.html.

8 Ibid.

8 Ibid.

8 Ibid.

8 Ma, "Horrifying Eyewitness Accounts."

13 Yousur Al-Hlou, "New ISIS Video on Paris Attacks," *New York Times,* January 25, 2016, https://www.nytimes.com/video/world /100000004166589/isis-video-appears-to-show-assailants.html.

13 Ibid.

15 Jethro Mullen and Margot Haddad, "'France Is at War,' President Francois Hollande Says after ISIS Attack," *CNN,* November 16, 2016, http://www.cnn.com/2015/11/16/world/paris-attacks/.

18 Joby Warrick, *Black Flags: The Rise of ISIS* (New York: Doubleday, 2015), 111.

24 Ibid., 45.

25 Ibid., 71.

25–26 Malise Ruthven, "Inside the Islamic State," *New York Review of Books,* July 9, 2015, http://www.nybooks.com/articles/2015/07/09 /inside-islamic-state/.

26 Jim Muir, "Islamic State Group: The Full Story," *BBC News,* June 20, 2016, http://www.bbc.com/news/world-middle-east-35695648.

28 David Kilcullen, *Blood Year: The Unraveling of Western Counterterrorism* (New York: Oxford University Press, 2016), 32.

30 "The Official Website of the Amman Message," Amman Message, accessed February 12, 2017, http://ammanmessage.com.

30 Warrick, *Black Flags,* 157.

31 Ibid., 248.

33 David Denby, "The Perfect Children of ISIS: Lessons from Dabiq," *New Yorker,* November 24, 2015, http://www.newyorker.com /culture/cultural-comment/the-perfect-children-of-isis-lessons -from-dabiq.

36 C. J. Chivers, "Behind the Black Flag: The Recruitment of an ISIS Killer," *New York Times,* December 20, 2015, https://www.nytimes .com/2015/12/21/world/middleeast/isis-recruitment-killer-hassan -aboud.html.

38 Anand Gopol, "The Hell after ISIS," *Atlantic,* May 2016, http://www .theatlantic.com/magazine/archive/2016/05/the-hell-after-isis /476391/.

39 Ibid.

39 Ibid.

40 "The Rise of Isis," *Frontline,* October 28, 2014, http://www.pbs.org /wgbh/frontline/film/rise-of-isis/.

40 Mike Shum, Greg Campbell, Adam B. Ellick, and Mona El-Naggar, "Surviving an ISIS Massacre," *New York Times,* September 4, 2014, https://www.nytimes.com/video/world/middleeast /100000003077656/surviving-isis-massacre-iraq.html.

41 Ibid.

42 Uri Friedman, "Obama Confronts the Joker of the Middle East," *Atlantic*, March 10, 2016, http://www.theatlantic.com/notes/2016 /03/obama-isis-joker-batman/473193/.

42 Shreeya Sinha, "Obama's Evolution on ISIS," *New York Times,* June 9, 2015, https://www.nytimes.com/interactive/2015/06/09/world /middleeast/obama-isis-strategy.html.

43 Graeme Wood, "What ISIS Really Wants," *Atlantic,* March 2015, http://www.theatlantic.com/magazine/archive/2015/03/what-isis -really-wants/384980/.

43 Warrick, *Black Flags,* 304–305.

44 Ibid., 305.

46 Erika Solomon, "Escape from ISIS," *Financial Times,* January 29, 2016, https://www.ft.com/content/3afe4c80-c534-11e5-b3b1 -7b2481276e45.

46 Ibid.

47 Ibid.

47 Rukmini Callimachi, "To Maintain Supply of Sex Slaves, ISIS Pushes Birth Control," *New York Times,* March 12, 2016, https://www .nytimes.com/2016/03/13/world/middleeast/to-maintain-supply -of-sex-slaves-isis-pushes-birth-control.html.

48 Jeffrey Goldberg, "The Obama Doctrine," *Atlantic,* April 2016, https://www.theatlantic.com/magazine/archive/2016/04/the-obama-doctrine/471525/.

49 Lyse Doucet, "How Four Men Survived as Hostages of IS," *BBC News*, April 20, 2016, http://www.bbc.com/news/magazine-36080991.

49 Ibid.

50 Lawrence Wright, "Five Hostages," *New Yorker,* July 6 and 13, 2015, http://www.newyorker.com/magazine/2015/07/06/five-hostages.

50 Ibid.

52 Robert Worth, *A Rage for Order: The Middle East in Turmoil, from Tahrir Square to ISIS* (New York: Farrar, Straus & Giroux, 2016), 177.

53 David Remnick, "Telling the Truth about Raqqa and ISIS," *New Yorker,* November 22, 2015, http://www.newyorker.com/news/news-desk/telling-the-truth-about-isis-and-raqqa.

53 Worth, *Rage for Order,* 178–179.

53 Gopol, "The Hell after ISIS."

53 Remnick, "Telling the Truth."

54 William McCants, "How ISIS Got Its Flag," *Atlantic,* September 22, 2015, https://www.theatlantic.com/international/archive/2015/09/isis-flag-apocalypse/406498/.

54 Ben Taub, "Journey to Jihad," *New Yorker,* June 1, 2015, http://www.newyorker.com/magazine/2015/06/01/journey-to-jihad.

54 Remnick, "Telling the Truth."

54 Ibid.

55 Ibid.

55 Nabeelah Shaikh, Amanda Khoza, and Charmel Payet, "'SA' Man's Isis Video Probed," *IOL,* August 17, 2014, http://www.iol.co.za/news/politics/sa-mans-isis-video-probed-1736583.

56–57 Scott Anderson, "Fractured Lands: How the Arab World Came Apart," *New York Times,* August 10, 2016, https://www.nytimes.com/interactive/2016/08/11/magazine/isis-middle-east-arab-spring-fractured-lands.html.

57 Scott Shane, "From Minneapolis to ISIS: An American's Path to Jihad," *New York Times,* March 21, 2015, https://www.nytimes.com/2015/03/22/world/middleeast/from-minneapolis-to-isis-an-americans-path-to-jihad.html.

57 Cody M. Poplin and Sebastian Brady, "The ISIS Guide to Holy War, or Lonely Planet: Islamic State," *Lawfare* (blog), March 27, 2015,

https://www.lawfareblog.com/isis-guide-holy-war-or-lonely-planet-islamic-state.

58 Robin Wright, "Is the Islamic State Hurting? The President's Point Man on ISIS Speaks Out," *New Yorker,* March 3, 2016, http://www.newyorker.com/news/news-desk/is-the-islamic-state-hurting-the-presidents-point-man-on-isis-speaks-out.

58 Peter Bergen, "ISIS Online: Countering Terrorist Radicalization and Recruitment on the Internet and Social Media," US Senate Committee on Homeland Security, July 6, 2016, http://www.hsgac.senate.gov/download/bergen-testimony_psi-2016-07-05.

58 Ibid.

59 Thomas Hegghammer, "The Soft Power of Militant Jihad," *New York Times,* December 18, 2015, https://www.nytimes.com/2015/12/20/opinion/sunday/militant-jihads-softer-side.html.

59 Ibid.

59 Ibid.

60 Janet Reitman, "The Children of ISIS," *Rolling Stone,* March 25, 2015, http://www.rollingstone.com/culture/features/teenage-jihad-inside-the-world-of-american-kids-seduced-by-isis-20150325.

60 Ibid.

60 Worth, *Rage for Order,* 184.

60 Ibid.

61 Ibid., 186.

61 Ibid.

62 "Dabiq: Why Is Syrian Town So Important for IS," *BBC News,* October 4, 2016, http://www.bbc.com/news/world-middle-east-30083303.

63 Worth, *Rage for Order,* 186.

63 Ibid.

65 Malise Ruthven, "Lure of the Caliphate," *New York Review of Books,* February 25, 2015, http://www.nybooks.com/daily/2015/02/28/lure-caliphate-isis/.

66 Ibid.

66 Ibid.

66 Oasis, *Ils cherchent le paradis, ils ont trouvé l'enfer,* book review, Oasis, March 4, 2015, http://www.oasiscenter.eu/reviews/2015/03/04/with-isis-because-i-love-death-more-than-you-love-life.

69 "Islamic State Blows Up Ancient Arch of Triumph in Palmyra," Jihad Watch, October 5, 2015, https://www.jihadwatch.org/2015/10 /islamic-state-blows-up-ancient-arch-of-triumph-in-palmyra.

70 Bergen, "ISIS Online."

70 Ibid.

70 Ibid.

71 Ellie Hall, "Gone Girl: An Interview with an American Girl in ISIS," *BuzzFeed,* April 17, 2015, https://www.buzzfeed.com/ellievhall/gone -girl-an-interview-with-an-american-in-isis?utm_term=.fbNOEPvMp #.lpBpjRkB6.

71 Ibid.

71 Scott Shane, Matt Apuzzo, and Eric Schmitt, "Americans Attracted to ISIS Find an 'Echo Chamber' on Social Media," *New York Times,* December 8, 2015, https://www.nytimes.com/2015/12/09/us /americans-attracted-to-isis-find-an-echo-chamber-on-social -media.html.

72 Laura King, Nabih Bulos, and W. J. Hennigan, "Why Islamic State's Abu Muhammad Adnani Was Much More Than a Spokesman," *Los Angeles Times,* August 30, 2016, http://www.latimes.com/world/la -fg-islamic-state-spokesman-killed-20160830-snap-story.html.

72–73 Justin Wingerter, "John Booker Jr. Pleads Guilty to Terrorism Charges Stemming from 2015 Fort Riley Bomb Plot," *Topeka Capital-Journal,* February 3, 2016, http://cjonline.com/news-local /2016-02-03/john-booker-jr-pleads-guilty-terrorism-charges -stemming-2015-fort-riley-bomb.

74 Les Neuhaus, "Pulse D.J.s Recall How Joyful Beats Gave Way to Massacre Gunfire," *New York Times,* June 18, 2016, https://www .nytimes.com/2016/06/19/us/pulse-djs-recall-how-joyful-beats -gave-way-to-massacre-gunfire.html.

74 Jack Healy and Marc Santora, "Held Hostage in an Orlando Restroom, and Playing Dead to Stay Alive," *New York Times,* June 13, 2016, https://www.nytimes.com/2016/06/14/us/reconstruct -orlando-pulse-shootings.html?_r=0.

74–75 Frances Robles, "'I Thought They Were Playing Dead': Officers Are Haunted by Scene at Orlando Club," *New York Times,* June 23, 2016, https://www.nytimes.com/2016/06/24/us/i-thought-they -were-playing-dead-officers-are-haunted-by-scene-at-orlando-club .html.

75 "Investigative Update Regarding Pulse Nightclub Shooting," FBI, June 20, 2016, https://www.fbi.gov/contact-us/field-offices/tampa /news/press-releases/investigative-update-regarding-pulse -nightclub-shooting.

80 "The Human Toll of Terror," *New York Times,* July 26, 2016, https://www.nytimes.com/interactive/2016/07/27/world/human-toll-of-terror-attacks.html.

80 Alissa Rubin and Aurelien Breeden, "ISIS Claims Truck Attacker in France Was Its 'Soldier,'" *New York Times,* July 16, 2016, https://www.nytimes.com/2016/07/17/world/europe/isis-nice-france-attack.html.

82 Tim Hains, "Trump's Updated ISIS Plan: 'Bomb the Shit out of Them,' Send in Exxon to Rebuild," *Real Clear Politics,* November 13, 2015, http://www.realclearpolitics.com/video/2015/11/13/trumps_updated_isis_plan_bomb_the_shit_out_of_them_send_exxon_in_to_rebuild.html.

83 Karen McVeigh, "Drone Strikes: Tears in Congress as Pakistani Family Tells of Mother's Death," *Guardian* (US ed.), October 29, 2013, https://www.theguardian.com/world/2013/oct/29/pakistan-family-drone-victim-testimony-congress.

83 Ibid.

84–85 Kelsey Snell and Abby Phillip, "McConnell: We Don't Have Religious Tests in This Country," *Washington Post,* January 29, 2017, https://www.washingtonpost.com/powerpost/mcconnell-we-dont-have-religious-tests-in-this-country/2017/01/29/03215604-e630-11e6-b82f-687d6e6a3e7c_story.html?utm_term=.e6e96714f03b.

85 Clive Crook, "What the West Doesn't Get about Terror," *Bloomberg,* July 19, 2016, https://www.bloomberg.com/view/articles/2016-07-19/what-the-west-doesn-t-get-about-terror.

85 Melissa Bell, Saskya Vandoorne, and Bryony Jones, "Marine Le Pen: Impossible Made Possible by Trump Win," *CNN,* November 27, 2016, http://www.cnn.com/2016/11/15/politics/marine-le-pen-interview-donald-trump/.

88 Hassan Hassan, "Is the Islamist State Unstoppable?," *New York Times,* July 9, 2016, https://www.nytimes.com/2016/07/10/opinion/is-the-islamic-state-unstoppable.html.

88 Ibid.

89 Joseph Goldstein, "Defeat of ISIS Could Send 'Terrorist Diaspora' to West, FBI Chief Says," *New York Times,* July 27, 2016, https://www.nytimes.com/2016/07/28/world/isis-attacks.html.

GLOSSARY

apocalypse: a final battle between good and evil as predicted in many religious texts. According to Islamic teaching, the apocalypse will occur after a period of injustice against Muslims, who will then be united by a caliph. Islamic texts say that the battle will take place at Dabiq, Syria, and that an era of peace and righteousness will follow.

apostasy: the act of gravely contradicting religious teaching. In Islam, apostasy is a very serious charge, punishable by death. A person who engages in apostasy is called an apostate.

caliph: a successor of Muhammad who serves at the spiritual head of Islam. In June 2014, ISIS leader Abu Bakr al-Baghdadi declared a new caliphate based in Syria and Iraq and designated himself caliph.

caliphate: a territory ruled by a successor to Muhammad, governed under sharia law.

crucifixion: a killing carried out by binding someone's hands and feet to a large cross. Victims of crucifixion die slowly, usually by asphyxiation, because hanging by one's hands from a cross makes breathing increasingly difficult. ISIS uses crucifixion and other punishments commonly used during the time of Muhammad.

genocide: the deliberate and systematic killing of members of a certain racial, political, religious, or cultural group. The international community called ISIS's killing of five thousand Yazidi men in 2014 a genocide.

insurgency: a movement to overthrow a government or occupying power. After the United States invaded Iraq in 2003, many Iraqis joined an insurgency against occupying US forces.

ISIS: a terrorist organization based in Syria and Iraq that vows to wage jihad, or holy war, against anyone who does not adhere to its extremist interpretation of Islam. ISIS has committed or inspired hundreds of terrorist attacks worldwide and has enslaved or murdered thousands.

Islam: a religion founded by the prophet Muhammad in the seventh century CE on the Arabian Peninsula. Shortly after its founding, Islam split into two sects, the Sunnis and Shiites. Members of ISIS belong to the Sunni branch of Islam.

jihad: a holy war waged against the enemies of Islam. ISIS wages jihad against non-Muslims as well as Muslims who don't adhere to its strict interpretation of Islam.

martyr: a person who sacrifices his or her life for a cause. According to ISIS's worldview, those who martyr themselves for the cause of jihad will enter paradise, or heaven, after death.

mujahideen: Islamic jihadists fighting in the Middle East. The term was widely used in the 1980s to describe jihadists fighting against Soviet troops in Afghanistan, but ISIS fighters sometimes also refer to themselves as mujahideen.

Quran: the holy book of Islam. Muslims believe that the angel Gabriel revealed the book to the prophet Muhammad in the seventh century CE. They believe that Allah, or God, sent the book to Muhammad as a guide for humans to live by.

sharia law: Islamic law as written in the Quran, the Muslim holy book, and in the hadith, a collection of writings about the words and deeds of Muhammed. ISIS strictly follows sharia law in business, warfare, and family life.

Shiites: members of one of the two major branches of Islam. Shiites believe that only a direct descendant of Muhammad can lead the Muslim community. In the twenty-first century, Shiites make up about 10 percent of the world's Muslim population. ISIS, which is composed of Sunni Muslims, view Shiites as apostates.

Sunnis: members of one of the two major branches of Islam. Sunnis do not believe that leaders of the Islamic community need to be direct descendants of Muhammad. Sunnis tend to interpret the teachings of Muhammad more literally than do Shiites. Members of ISIS belong to the Sunni branch of Islam.

surveillance: close watch kept over people by a government, another authority, or another individual. The US government carries out heavy surveillance of US and international Internet traffic in an effort to detect and monitor terrorist activity.

terrorism: the use of violence or the threat of violence to create fear and alarm among a civilian population. ISIS uses terror tactics such as bombings, mass shootings, and suicide attacks against those it views as enemies and infidels.

West: the democratic, industrialized nations of western Europe and North America, as well as other nations (such as Australia) that share their political and social values. ISIS opposes Western traditions, such as democratic governance and rights for women.

SELECTED BIBLIOGRAPHY

Armstrong, Karen. *Islam: A Short History.* New York: Modern Library, 2000.

Bergen, Peter. *United States of Jihad.* New York: Crown, 2016.

Denby, David. "The Perfect Children of ISIS: Lessons from Dabiq." *New Yorker,* November 24, 2015. http://www.newyorker.com/culture /cultural-comment/the-perfect-children-of-isis-lessons-from-dabiq.

Finnegan, William. "Last Days: Preparing for the Apocalypse in San Bernardino." *New Yorker,* February 22, 2016. http://www.newyorker .com/magazine/2016/02/22/preparing-for-apocalypse-in-san -bernardino.

Gerges, Fawaz A. *Isis: A History.* Princeton, NJ: Princeton University Press, 2016.

Hall, Ellie. "Gone Girl: An Interview with an American Girl in ISIS." *BuzzFeed,* April 17, 2015. https://www.buzzfeed.com/ellievhall/gone-girl-an -interview-with-an-american-in-isis?utm_term=.fbNOEPvMp#.lpBpjRkB6.

Hassan, Hassan. "Is the Islamist State Unstoppable?" *New York Times,* July 9, 2016. https://www.nytimes.com/2016/07/10/opinion/is-the-islamic -state-unstoppable.html.

Hegghammer, Thomas. "The Soft Power of Militant Jihad." *New York Times,* December 18, 2015. https://www.nytimes.com/2015/12/20/opinion /sunday/militant-jihads-softer-side.html.

Kilcullen, David. *Blood Year: The Unraveling of Western Counterterrorism.* New York: Oxford University Press, 2016.

Nance, Malcolm. *Defeating ISIS: Who They Are, How They Fight, What They Believe.* New York: Skyhorse, 2016.

Reitman, Janet. "The Children of ISIS." *Rolling Stone,* March 25, 2015. http:// www.rollingstone.com/culture/features/teenage-jihad-inside-the-world -of-american-kids-seduced-by-isis-20150325.

Taub, Ben. "Journey to Jihad." *New Yorker,* June 1, 2015. http://www .newyorker.com/magazine/2015/06/01/journey-to-jihad.

Wood, Graeme. "What ISIS Really Wants." *Atlantic,* March 2015. http:// www.theatlantic.com/magazine/archive/2015/03/what-isis-really -wants/384980/.

Worth, Robert. *A Rage for Order: The Middle East in Turmoil, from Tahrir Square to ISIS.* New York: Farrar, Straus & Giroux, 2016.

Wright, Lawrence. "Five Hostages." *New Yorker,* July 6 and 13, 2015. http:// www.newyorker.com/magazine/2015/07/06/five-hostages.

FURTHER INFORMATION

Books

Di Giovanni, Janine. *The Morning They Came for Us: Dispatches from Syria.* New York: Liveright, 2016.

Kennan, Caroline. *The Rise of Isis: The Modern Age of Terrorism.* Farmington Hills, MI: Lucent, 2017.

McCants, William. *The ISIS Apocalypse: The History, Strategy, and Doomsday Vision of the Islamic State.* New York: St. Martin's, 2015.

Netzley, Patricia D. *Terrorism and War of the 2000s.* San Diego: ReferencePoint, 2014.

Stern, Jessica, and J. M. Berger. *ISIS: The State of Terror.* New York: Ecco, 2015.

Sullivan, Anne Marie. *Syria.* Broomall, PA: Mason Crest, 2015.

Thompson, Bill, and Dorcas Thompson. *Iraq.* Broomall, PA: Mason Crest, 2015.

Warrick, Joby. *Black Flags: The Rise of ISIS.* New York: Doubleday, 2015.

Weiss, Michael, and Hassan Hassan. *ISIS: Inside the Army of Terror.* New York: Regan Arts, 2015.

Wright, Lawrence. *The Terror Years: From al-Qaeda to the Islamic State.* New York: Knopf, 2016.

Films

The Rise of ISIS. DVD. Arlington, VA: Public Broadcasting Service, 2014.
This documentary film explores how ISIS arose in Iraq during the Iraq War, how the terrorist organization has grown since then, and the threat it poses in the Middle East and beyond.

The Secret History of ISIS. DVD. Arlington, VA: Public Broadcasting Service, 2012.
This video takes viewers inside the ISIS organization. It tells the story of the radicals who founded the group and shows how the United States missed important red flags as the group became more powerful.

Syria's Second Front. DVD. Arlington, VA: Public Broadcasting Service, 2014.
This documentary details how rebels fighting the Bashar Assad regime in Syria have radicalized and splintered into factions. Many of these groups have aligned themselves with ISIS.

Wounds of Waziristan. DVD. New York: Madiha Tahir and Parergon Films, 2013.

The United States uses drones to attack ISIS and other terrorist organizations in the Middle East. However, such air strikes frequently kill innocent civilians. This documentary film describes the horrors endured by Pakistani victims of US drone strikes.

Websites

The Islamic State

http://www.cfr.org/iraq/islamic-state/p14811

This website from the Council on Foreign Relations, a US-based think tank and publisher, provides a deep background on ISIS, how it grew, and where it might be headed. The site also discusses what Western nations are doing to fight ISIS.

Islamic State Group: The Full Story

http://www.bbc.com/news/world-middle-east-35695648

The British Broadcasting Corporation site provides an in-depth history of ISIS. The site also explores ISIS's leadership, its connection to other terrorist organizations, its philosophy and vision, and how it finances its activities.

The Islamic State's Magazine

http://www.clarionproject.org/news/islamic-state-isis-isil-propaganda-magazine-dabiq

Every issue of ISIS's *Dabiq* magazine and its newer *Rumiyah* magazine is available at this website, which is hosted by the Clarion Project. The magazine articles provide insights into ISIS's worldview and how it justifies its violent acts.

What Is ISIS?

http://www.teenvogue.com/story/isis-explainer

This website from *Teen Vogue* explains the nuts and bolts of ISIS's worldview and activities. The site also includes a video about how ISIS uses social media to recruit US teenagers.

INDEX

Afghanistan
  jihadist activities in, 20–21, 24–25
Amman Message, 30
antiquities and looting by ISIS, 13, 42,
    60, 69
apocalypse, 62
apostasy, 27
Arab Spring, 34, 38
Assad, Bashar, 35–36

Baghdad, Iraq, 16–18, 28, 80
Baghdadi, Abu Bakr al-, 32, 37, 42–44
beheadings, 12–13, 30, 50
bin Laden, Osama, 10, 24, 29
Bush, George W., 17

caliphate, 11, 20, 52
  creation of by Abu Bakr al-Baghdadi,
    43, 52
  of earlier eras, 44
Camp Bucca, 32
Comey, James B., 88–89
cultural monuments
  destruction of by ISIS, 68–69

Dabiq, 58
Dabiq, Syria, 62
drone strikes against terrorists
  civilian deaths by, 83

Emwazi, Mohammed (Jihadi John), 12,
    50–51
Europe, 10
  and Syrian refugees, 78–79, 85
  tensions between Muslims and non-
    Muslims in, 30, 71

Hussein, Saddam. *See* Saddam Hussein

Iraq, 17
  insurgency in, 18–19, 28, 31–33
  ISIS activities in, 14, 38–42
  sectarian violence in, 27–29, 44–47
Iraq War, 16–17, 26, 36
Islam
  history of, 9–10, 24, 62
  ISIS's interpretation of, 10–11, 44–45,
    53, 69

  sects of, 26–27
Islamic State in Iraq and Syria (ISIS)
  and child soldiers, 55
  executions by, 12–13, 39–41, 50–51, 62
  financing of, 12–13, 42
  flag of, 52–53
  formation of, 10, 37–38
  kidnappings by, 28, 42
  member recruitment, 11, 50–53,
    55–60, 64, 70–71
  names for, 10
  terrorist activities of, 4–9, 14, 39–41,
    44–50, 68–69, 79–81
  use of media, 65, 71–72
  women in, 54, 59–60

Jihadi John. *See* Emwazi, Mohammed
    (Jihadi John)

Khansaa Brigade, al-, 54

Le Pen, Marine, 85
lone-wolf attacks, 72–74

Maliki, Nouri al-, 28
maps, 9, 21
Maqdisi, Abu Muhammad al-, 22, 27
martyrdom, 63, 70–71
Mosul, Iraq
  battles for, 39–41
Muhammad, 10–11, 24, 26, 42–43,
    53–54

National Security Agency (NSA), 86

Obama, Barack, 36, 42, 48, 82
Ottoman Empire, 20, 43

Palmyra, Syria, 68–69
Paris, France
  ISIS attack on, 4–10, 13
Pulse nightclub
  lone-wolf attack on, 74–77

Qaeda, al-, 10, 16, 24–25, 36–37
Quran, 10, 22, 32

Raqqa, Syria, 52–55
recruitment strategies, 11, 55–60,
    64–65, 70–72

refugees from Syria, 78–79

Saddam Hussein, 16–18, 26–27
San Bernardino, California
   lone-wolf attack on, 73–74
September 11 (9/11) terrorist attacks,
   16–17, 25
sharia law, 10–11, 21, 33, 53, 55, 79
Shiites, 26–29, 38
Soviet Union
   military involvement in Afghanistan,
      20, 88
   military involvement in Syria, 35
suicide bombings, 5, 27, 31, 39, 70,
   79–80
Sunnis, 26–29, 38–39
surveillance of terrorist activities, 30–31
   and privacy of US citizens, 86
Syria, 68
   civil war in, 11, 34–36
   ISIS activities in, 14, 36–37, 42, 52–55,
      69
   refugees from, 78–79

Taliban, 21, 24
Trump, Donald, 82, 84–87
Turkey
   ISIS attacks in, 80
   and ISIS recruits crossing border, 57,
      65, 70

United States
   air strikes, 48, 82
   attitudes about Islam, 30, 79, 84–85
   and Iraq War, 11, 16–18, 36
   ISIS-inspired attacks in, 16–17, 72–76,
      74–77
   ISIS recruits in, 70–71
   policies toward Muslim immigrants,
      84–85
   and surveillance of citizens, 86
   and Syrian civil war, 35–36

West
   demonization of by ISIS, 10–11, 50, 70
   and historical dominance of Middle
      East, 20–21, 33
women
   in ISIS's ranks, 54, 59–60
   ISIS's treatment of, 10, 45–47, 53–54

Yazidis
   enslavement of women by ISIS, 46–47
   ISIS attack on, 44–45
   massacre of men by ISIS, 46–47

Zarqawi, Abu Musab al-, 18–31

PHOTO ACKNOWLEDGMENTS

The images in this book are used with the permission of:
Background: Ensuper/Shutterstock.com; REUTERS/Christian Hartmann,
p. 4; © Laura Westlund/Independent Picture Service, pp. 9, 21; HO/EyePress
EPN/Collection/Newscom, p. 12; © STEPHANE DE SAKUTIN/AFP/Getty
Images, p. 14; © Gilles BASSIGNAC/Gamma-Rapho/Getty Images, p. 16;
REUTERS/Suhaib Salem, p. 19; © Arab TV Network/ZUMA Press, p. 23;
© 0851/GAMMA/Gamma-Rapho/Getty Images, p. 29; © Si Mitchell/
AFP/Getty Images, p. 34; © 2016 Anadolu Agency/Getty Images, p. 37;
REUTERS/Stringer, pp. 41, 56; © ADAM FERGUSON/The New York Times/
Redux, p. 45; Handout/Alamy Stock Photo, p. 52; © Huseyin Nasir/Anadolu
Agency/Getty Images, p. 62; © REX/Shutterstock, pp. 64, 68; © William
Van Hecke/Corbis/Getty Images, p. 67; REUTERS/Mike Blake, p. 74;
© Samuel Corum/Anadolu Agency/Getty Images, p. 76; Craig Stennett/
Alamy Stock Photo, p. 78; © AHMAD AL-RUBAYE/AFP/Getty Images, p. 81;
© Ethan Miller/Getty Images, p. 83; a katz/Shutterstock.com, p. 84; © Drew
Angerer/Getty Images, p. 87.

Front cover: © Vakabungo/Dreamstime.com (knife); Ensuper/Shutterstock.
com (grunge texture).

ABOUT THE AUTHOR

Brendan January is an award-winning author of more than twenty nonfiction books for young readers, including the 2016 title *Information Insecurity: Privacy under Siege.* He attended Haverford College and the Columbia University Graduate School of Journalism and was a Fulbright scholar in Germany. He lives with his wife and two children in Maplewood, New Jersey.